# Risen from the Ashes

## Tales of a Musical Messenger

Hans Cohn

**Hamilton Books**
A member of
The Rowman & Littlefield Publishing Group
*Lanham • Boulder • New York • Toronto • Oxford*

**Copyright © 2006 by**
**Hamilton Books**
4501 Forbes Boulevard
Suite 200
Lanham, Maryland 20706
Hamilton Books Acquisitions Department (301) 459-3366

PO Box 317
Oxford
OX2 9RU, UK

Library of Congress Control Number: 2005932383
ISBN 0-7618-3283-1 (paperback : alk. ppr.)

 ™ The paper used in this publication meets the minimum
requirements of American National Standard for Information
Sciences—Permanence of Paper for Printed Library Materials,
ANSI Z39.48—1992

Dedicated to the memory of the stateless refugees of the Shanghai ghetto who escaped and survived the Nazi horror. May they never be forgotten.

# Table of Contents

# Acknowledgements

Writing this book was therapy in surviving my bout with throat cancer. After the loss of my beloved wife Eva, I spent the lonely evenings reliving my past. Although she is not physically with me to share the sunset of my life, I feel her spiritual presence which pervades throughout the book.

Thanks to my three daughters Becki, Ruth, and Barbara who stood by my side to support me in my grief—they were my blessings. I am indebted to June Brott, my outstanding editor whose professional expertise in making suggestions and spending hours on the phone.

I am most grateful to Professor Lee Shulman, Rabbi Michael Berenbaum, Marsha Lee Berkman, Bruno Wassertheil, Rena Krasno, and Bernard Sheier for reading the manuscript and their helpful advice. My heartfelt thanks go to Barbara Noble, the instructor of the Palo Alto Writer's Club and to its members who encouraged and challenged me to tell my story. To John and Mary Louise Jaffray, for reviewing the manuscript for syntax. To Molly Landers, whose computer skills helped me to put the final touches on the book for publication. To Nina Lobban, my faithful companion, for her assistance in proofreading and in organizing the material.

Last but not least, to the many friends who read sample chapters. I benefited greatly from their critique. In writing these chapters I look ahead to a brighter future to someday leave this world better than I found it.

# EARLY YEARS

# Chapter One

# Déjà Vu

I was feeling especially good on the Shabbat of February 3, 1979. As I drove home from Temple Beth Jacob, I thought again how lucky I was to be a cantor, a job that meant much more to me than just earning a livelihood. I was doing what I loved most—singing, praying, and teaching children. That morning the children's Sabbath services had gone especially well. I was beaming with pride at how beautifully the students of my Junior Congregation led the prayers. Continuing on into the main sanctuary, I felt in excellent voice and led the adult service with vigor and joy.

About one o'clock I came home, still exhilarated, and began a leisurely winter lunch with my wife, Eva. After enjoying a steaming bowl of noodle soup, challah, and chicken warmed-over from Friday night, I was relaxed and grateful for not having to run off again to some Temple activity. With pleasure I looked forward to my regular Shabbat afternoon nap in a totally quiet house since friends and congregants never telephoned until after sunset.

About three o'clock I stretched out on the living room couch and began browsing through the newspaper, not getting very far before gently drifting off into a refreshing rest. But my deep dream world was cut short.

"Hans!" Eva nudged me. "You didn't hear the phone ring? It's only four o'clock but it must be urgent! Hans, someone sounds frantic!"

"Who is it?" I mumbled into the receiver, half-asleep and somewhat annoyed to be called before dark.

"Cantor! Our Temple is on fire!" cried the tear-choked caller, a student who lived near the temple. "Come quickly!" he pleaded.

Fully awake but in disbelief, I bolted up from the couch and dashed into my car. It was not quite dusk when I set out. Ignoring speed limits, the usual twenty-minute ride took just fifteen, thanks to light traffic. By the time I reached Beth Jacob, it was almost dark and I was breathless with anxiety. I was met by a distressed Dr. Norman Stone, our president, and Joe Aknin, a member who lived down the street.

The temple was ablaze, totally engulfed in flames, and we were all in a state of despair. As crackling fire gutted the building, my first thought was to get to the Holy Ark and save our precious Torah scrolls. Roaring flames shot up against the now dark sky, bringing back shocking memories. As if in a replay of my youth from Germany, I was again witnessing the terrible scene of the Berlin temple my family attended being destroyed in a horrendous fire on November 9, 1938.

On that night—*Kristallnacht*—the Nazis burned all the synagogues in Berlin as well as all over Germany and Austria. I vividly remembered our Berlin cantor courageously entering the burning structure, attempting to save Judaism's Written Law, the hand-lettered parchment scrolls of the Torah. As cantor of Beth Jacob I wanted to do the same thing, so with the help of a fireman, I donned a helmet, braced for a serious risk, and entered the flaming building.

Unfortunately, it was of no avail. The contents of the ark were beyond saving. The silver vestments, crowns, breastplate and pointers that once adorned the Torahs had completely melted. All I could rescue were the charred remains of the scrolls. In the blackness of the crumbling sanctuary, I fell, sprained my ankle and injured my knee. Limping into the school wing, however, I was able to save a single Torah, the one our Junior Congregation had used that very morning.

As temple members began hearing the terrible news on the radio, they rushed to the scene and watched helplessly. With tears in their eyes they stood for two hours in the chill of the February night, seeking warmth by embracing each other. Attempting to put out the flames, three firemen were injured and taken to the hospital. I recalled the German firemen standing by my burning synagogue with their hoses but doing nothing. They were interested only in preventing any damage to the nearby Berlin homes.

The next day, Sunday, in the smoldering ruins of the temple, Rabbi Teitelbaum and I—hobbling on crutches—conducted services for the dazed, stunned congregation. By daylight it was possible to survey the damage. The sanctuary, social hall, choir room, and kitchen were totally destroyed. The organ and the piano were piles of ashes.

All three local TV networks reported on the disastrous fire. When interviewed, I mentioned that in the past we had received some anti-Semitic hate mail and threats as well as a small fire set in one of the garbage cans. But the conflagration on February 3, 1979 was a shocking calamity for all Temple Beth Jacob members. For me, however, it was déjà vu.

## Chapter Two

# A Time to be Born

I sometimes wonder what would have become of me had my mother married Franz. He was a handsome, well-built German gentile and a decorated World War I veteran. A cultured young man, Franz prided himself on his noble heritage.

My mother—Ida Graupner—was a charming brunette. She was slender, outgoing, and vivacious. The two hit it off well, sharing many common interests. One Sunday in spring they planned a picnic in the *Grunewald*, a picturesque forested area on the outskirts of Berlin. A lover of nature, my mother was in excellent spirits.

"I'm delighted we decided to come here. It's a perfect day," she raved to Franz.

"Well, I'd enjoy it much more," he retorted, "if there weren't so damned many Jews around here."

As though struck by lightning, my mother's heart stopped. She did not look Jewish and her name was not Jewish, but she was nevertheless insulted and angered by Franz's unexpected remark.

"I am a Jew," she told him, "and I'm proud of it." Then she stood up, walked away, and never saw Franz again.

Soon after this disturbing experience, my mother attended a party in Berlin where she met Max Cohn, a salesman of men's clothing. She had a strong personality and Max was unassuming and rather quiet, so they suited each other very well. Before long they fell in love and in 1920 were united in a simple wedding ceremony in Rabbi Warschauer's office.

The times then were very unsettled. Since 1918 when Germany lost the First World War, dark clouds had hung over Berlin as well as the whole country. The war, a calamitous event that threw the whole world into ferment, began with two shots from an assassin's pistol. On July 28, 1914 a Serbian anarchist, Gavrilo Princip, killed Crown Prince Archduke Francis Ferdinand and his wife Sophie while the couple was visiting Sarajevo, the capital of Bosnia.

Ferdinand was the nephew of Emperor Franz Joseph of Austria-Hungary and heir to the throne. The Emperor, enraged after the assassination, declared war on Serbia and was joined by Germany, which had an alliance with the Austro-Hungarian Empire. This alliance, which marked the rise of nationalism and territorial expansion in Europe, was further strengthened when Kaiser Wilhelm II, the Emperor of Prussia, also declared war on Serbia.

Soon almost all of Europe was embroiled in a bloody battle between two camps The Central Powers included Austria, Germany, and Bulgaria, along with Turkey. The Allies, aiding Serbia, consisted of Russia, France, and England, as well as twenty-one other nations including the United States, which joined on April 6, 1917.

World War I was a battle of indescribable proportions with tanks, airplanes, and poison gas being used for the first time. In 1915 my father, a German citizen, became one of 100,000 Jewish volunteers who joined the German army to defend the *Vaterland* against the Allies. An infantry soldier, he fought valiantly, was wounded in the battle of Verdun, and proudly received the Iron Cross for bravery. Out of loyalty to the Prussian Empire approximately 12,000 Jews sacrificed their lives, a disproportionately high number of casualties. In 1914 Germany's Jewish population was only 615,000, less than one percent of the country's 60 million Germans.

In 1919 after Germany lost the war, a peace conference under the auspices of the League of Nations produced the Treaty of Versailles. Ratified in 1920, the treaty forced Germany to disarm, pay $32 billion in war reparations, give up her African colonies, and reduce her territory by returning parts of her land to France, Belgium, and Denmark.

The treaty resulted in some changes on the ground. Poland was given free access to the Baltic Sea. Known as the Polish Corridor, this access bisected East Prussia from Germany, causing Prussia's Emperor Wilhelm II to flee to Holland. The German city of Posen, where my father was born, became part of Poland and was re-named Poznan. Danzig or Gdansk was declared a "free city" to be under the supervision of the League of Nations. At the same time, Czechoslovakia, Hungary and Lithuania became independent countries. My father decided to leave Polish Poznan and he settled in Berlin.

In 1919 a new democratic government was formed—the Weimar Republic under Friedrich Ebert. In 1925 Paul von Hindenburg, a military leader who had commanded all German forces during the war, became the Weimar president. Germany faced serious problems in the years between the Weimar Republic and the Nazi Era, a period facetiously named "The Golden Twenties."

Unable to meet her financial obligation to pay war reparations, the country was beset by unemployment and starvation. Poverty was rampant. Runaway inflation made German currency worthless. A loaf of bread cost one million marks, then equivalent to an American dollar.

A climate of hatred and resentment filled the air. It was a perfect time for Adolf Hitler to incite a rebellion, which he did by blaming the Jews not only for Germany's defeat in the war, but also for the misery that followed. During this period Albert Einstein, the celebrated Nobel Prize physicist, visited Berlin. Witnessing the spread of anti-Semitism, he predicted in all earnestness, "I shall be forced to leave Germany within the next ten years." He was absolutely correct.

World War I—which President Wilson labeled "the war to end all wars"—not only brought the German and Prussian Empires to an end; it also sowed the seeds for World War II. It was during this turbulent era between two world wars that I arrived on May 31, 1926—the same year in which the *Hitler Jugend*, the Hitler Youth movement was inaugurated.

What a time to be born!

*Chapter Three*

# Childhood Years

By 1930 Germany's fledgling Weimar Republic was still in power and President Paul von Hindenburg was still at its helm. For the Jews it was, relatively, a calm and bearable time.

My parents and I were a typical Jewish, middle-class family. We lived in Alt Moabit, a blue-collar suburb in East Berlin. Our small, humble apartment was located on the third floor of a building without an elevator. My parents and I shared the bedroom although there was a folding partition that allowed them some privacy. Our neighbors, non-Jews, were friendly but somewhat distant. The apartment faced the courtyard where every so often musicians or singers would come to entertain. To show our appreciation for them, we threw down coins from the window.

My mother and father made a modest living from a haberdashery they owned in Wedding, a working district in Berlin. The store, within walking distance of our apartment, featured accessories for ladies such as dresses, blouses, stockings, and sewing notions including buttons, ribbons, and needles. Although my mother was quite cultured, she was also handy at needlework and stitching. In the back of the store, she did minor clothing alterations, using an old-fashioned Pfaff sewing machine with a foot-operated treadle.

I was an only child. After hoping in vain to add to our family, my parents acquired Rolf, our faithful shepherd dog, to keep me company. Our cramped apartment was too small to accommodate Rolf so we decided that his home would have to be located in the storeroom of our shop. During favorable weather Rolf would sit quietly in front of the store, on a leash, watching me while I was in a baby carriage. Although gentle and affectionate, Rolf was also a wonderful watchdog. In fact, his presence saved us ten percent in insurance premiums against robbery and theft.

Around my fourth birthday, I was sent during the week to a nearby Catholic nursery school while my parents were working. The principal, Sister Redempta, a friend of my mother, was a buxom, blue-eyed nun whose blonde hair was neatly tucked inside her religious habit. Sister Redempta often brought me to my parents' store at closing time, and Rolf warmly greeted both of us. She always called me Hansel after the well-known fairy tale about Hansel and Gretel.

When I think of Sister Redempta, a well-known song from the musical *South Pacific* comes to mind. The words of "You've Got to be Carefully Taught" convey the powerful message that children are not born hating. To Sister Redempta, discrimination did not exist, just tolerance and love, peace on earth, and good will toward man. Words of kindness emanated from her lips. Everyone knew I was Jewish, but I felt well accepted because she told us children that God loved all his creatures, and she showed her love for me by passionately emphasizing that Jesus was a Jew. Only later would I understand that I was, really, different from everyone else.

On Friday nights I attended Sabbath services with my parents in the local downtown synagogue. The Hebrew prayers chanted by the cantor did not, of course, resemble the songs the church ladies taught me. The first Christian ones I learned and enjoyed were "Silent Night" and "*O Tannenbaum wie gruen sind deine Blaetter*" (O Christmas tree, how green are your leaves). However, it was all music to my ears and I loved it.

I have vague memories of the terrible snowstorm that struck Berlin in the winter of 1929. Freezing temperatures practically paralyzed the city. In our kitchen, the water pipes burst, covering the floor with a layer of ice. Although too young for ice-skating, I thought it was quite amusing to slide from the stove to the breakfast table. Because my mother feared that the store would be even colder than our apartment, she insisted on taking Rolf home with us to prevent him from freezing to death.

Unfortunately, her good intention resulted in a disaster. On the one and only night Rolf stayed with us, our store was robbed and thieves took most of our merchandise. When my parents filed a claim with the insurance company, their case was taken to court.

"Where was your dog the night of the robbery?" asked the insurance lawyer.

"We took him home because of the inclement weather," explained my mother.

To our dismay, we lost the case, not recouping even a penny for the goods we had lost. Out of kindness, the insurance company paid the court costs for us. But we were broke and had to start all over. Soon after, my parents closed the store and sought an alternative way to make a living. My mother found a job as a secretary and my father worked selling men's clothing, as he had done before marrying.

Meanwhile, Germany's political situation was changing. In 1932 President Hindenburg at eighty-five was elected again and the Weimar Republic's precarious days were numbered. The infamous Joseph Goebbles, Hitler's companion and Minister for Propaganda, exploited the government's weakness to gain publicity that helped the rise of National Socialism. The Nazi party, which Hitler had founded in 1919, reared its ugly head and by 1932 exceeded 100,000 members.

After threats and invectives, the ailing and senile President Hindenburg appointed Hitler as chancellor. Taking over the German government in 1933, Hitler continued blaming the Jews and communists for Germany's defeat during the First World War and began spreading his doctrine of "Today Germany and tomorrow the world." Racism flared up with a vengeance.

Although I was just seven years old in 1933, I remember one evening standing with my parents in our dimly lit living room, peeking through the curtains at a passing torchlight parade. Marching in goose step to beating drums and blaring music, Hitler's gangs bellowed the "Horst Wessel Song." Wessel, a Nazi thug killed in a street fight with communists, had been transformed into a martyr. The song became so popular it almost replaced the German national anthem. Shouts of *Sieg Heil* rang out through the air. Germany's red, gold and black flags were replaced with swastika banners, unfurled in tribute to the self-proclaimed savior. Young brown-shirted German hoodlums with swastika insignias and daggers in their sheaths yelled *Juden raus!* (Out with the Jews!)

Shielded by my parents, I was too young to understand what was happening. Only later would I realize that my religion, my "contaminated" blood, my dark curly hair, my hazel eyes, and my circumcised penis did not fit the ideal Aryan model.

# Chapter Four

# The Olympics

When Berlin hosted the Olympics in 1936, I was ten years old. Nazi Germany extended a warm welcome mat to the hundreds of foreigners who came to attend those famous competitions. German citizens were portrayed as peaceful, sports-minded fans interested in creating a friendly international environment. Flags from all nations fluttered and a festive atmosphere prevailed in the city.

As part of the Nazi pretense that there were no political problems and everything was "normal," the frequent anti-Semitic incidents eased and Jews were allowed to enter the Olympic Games. I was fortunate to attend a soccer game in the newly erected Olympic stadium, which still stands intact today. To keep up with other sporting events I couldn't attend, I listened on my little crystal set, which I had built myself. I kept the set, a simple radio that didn't use electricity, hidden under my bed and tucked its earphones under my pillow. At night when my parents thought I was asleep, I secretly listened for the results of the competitions.

Jesse Owens, the black American athlete, won the Gold Medal and set a world record for the hundred-meter dash. Although it was the Hitler's custom to congratulate the winners, when it came to Owens, he simply walked out of the stadium. That stadium, which still stands today, was closed for the last few years, but was rededicated in July 2004 by Jesse Owens' granddaughter. She lit the Olympic flame as a symbol of freedom and democracy.

When the Olympics came to an end, so did the glimmer of respite and hope we Jews had briefly experienced. Then Hitler's policy of persecution not only resumed but intensified. Gangs of Hitler's hoodlums roamed the streets and shouted, "*Juden geht nach Palestina*" (Jews, go to Palestine!)

Since it was no longer safe to play outside, I spent much of my leisure time alone. Television did not yet exist, and the one telephone we had was out of bounds for me. However, I had much fun playing our old-fashioned gramophone, listening to classical music and my father's 78-rpm recordings—Viennese waltzes, operettas, and Enrico Caruso, one of the world's most famous tenors. I had to crank up the phonograph by hand and intermittently change the needle.

Although I loved the music, my true avocation at that point was reading. Cooped up at home while my parents worked, books became my companions. I enjoyed detective stories, mysteries, and studying world geography. *Emil und die Detective (Emil and the Detectives)* by the celebrated author Erich Kaestner was my favorite book. Imbued with a desire to see the world, I was thrilled with Jules Verne's classic *Around the World in Eighty Days*. I would get out my atlas, look at the map, and follow the story while my fingers did the traveling.

In those days babysitters were unheard of, so my parents never left me home alone in the evenings. Sometimes I spent the night at Aunt Else's house. She was my mother's sister and the widow of a well-known cantor and opera singer. Little did I imagine then that I would follow my uncle's footsteps some twenty years later.

Jews were forbidden to perform in public, so the synagogue became a concert hall. To this day, I still remember performances of the *Kulturbund Deutscher Juden* (German-Jewish Culture Society). Dr. Kurt Singer, a physician and fine musician, had established the Society in 1933 with permission from the Nazi government. Much of the programming, of course, was propaganda intended to portray Germans as open-minded people, but the concerts also provided Jewish artists an opportunity to earn a living. Sitting with my parents, I would often fall asleep, yet something must have rubbed off on me because my love for music and especially for Jewish music blossomed at an early age.

As German anti-Semitism continued unabated, many Jews thought about immigrating to Palestine, which became a British mandate after World War I. With a Jewish population of only 550,000, Palestine was the sole country eager to absorb European Jews. The British Colonial Government, which already restricted Jewish immigration, issued its "White Paper" in 1939, further limiting the Jewish quota to 75,000 over five years. The Arabs, who didn't want any Jews to immigrate, reluctantly agreed to this plan. The Jews, however, vehemently objected because that number was a mere pittance considering that millions of Jews were anxious to leave Germany.

Henrietta Szold, Zionist leader and founder of Hadassah, a Jewish women's organization, helped create *Youth Aliyah* in order to save European Jewish children from the Nazis. She came to Berlin to organize their emigration to Palestine, where they could be resettled, educated and trained in vocational schools. *Youth Aliyah* did rescue thousands of children who otherwise would have perished in the concentration camps.

It would have been possible for me to join this youth movement, but only without my parents, and since I was their only child, a separation would have been too painful. My mother, a determined lady with strong family ties, was quite adamant.

"We must stay together at all costs," she insisted. "Maybe some other country will open its doors to us." Her decision was final. We were a family unit and would remain together.

*Chapter Five*

# The Assault

Everyday life and everyday anti-Semitism became even more difficult after Hitler's government unanimously adopted the infamous Nuremberg Laws in September of 1935. Nonstop discrimination and segregation increased.

German Jews lost their citizenship and were deprived of livelihoods. Public servants lost their jobs. Artists were fired from the opera, theater, and concert halls. Hitler's Stormtroopers frequently paraded in the streets of Berlin. "Down with the Jews" was the order of the day. Theaters and coffeehouses posted signs: *Juden Unerwuenscht* (Jews not wanted).

After my parents gave up their haberdashery business, we moved to West Berlin, where the majority of the city's 170,000 Jews lived. There it became easier for me to find other Jewish playmates who had also been expelled from German public schools. I was confused about the events of the day, and at the age of ten, of course, couldn't understand the political situation. I wondered what I had done wrong to be forced to leave school? What had I done to deserve being treated like an outcast? Little did I know these were just the beginning of worse things to come.

I continued my elementary education in a private Jewish school. Instruction by the Jewish teachers was comparable, if not better than at my previous schools. Besides German, we studied English and French. In addition, we received a Jewish religious education and began to learn Hebrew. Sharing a common destiny, we students played together, and developed close ties.

When I became a teenager, my parents enrolled me in *Adass Jisroel School,* a private high school operated by the Orthodox *Mizrachi* movement. The school opened its door to the many other boys and girls who had been expelled. Under the leadership of Rabbi Ezra Munk, 700 students obtained the finest traditional Jewish education, studying and speaking modern Hebrew along with secular subjects. To this day I am thankful for receiving such a wonderful foundation of Judaic knowledge. I learned to say my daily prayers, which I have continued—praying three times a day, putting on *Tefillin* (phylacteries) and wearing a *Yarmulkeh* (skull cap) during worship.

The school, located on *Sigmundshof* 11, was near the famous *Tiergarten* Park adjacent to the Spree River. To get to my classes, I walked fifteen minutes and then caught a train for a half-hour ride. When it became more difficult and dangerous to travel, I was enrolled at the *Lucie Hartwich Schule*, a private school that rented weekday space from the *Prinzregentenstrasse Synagogue*, one of the newest in Berlin and just a ten-minute walk from my house. Mrs. Hartwich, the principal, became my beloved teacher. She taught English, French and my favorite subject—music—using her guitar. Today, when I play guitar, I still think of her.

After the Nuremberg laws in 1935, my family's movements in Berlin were restricted. It was more difficult to travel, we could no longer go to a movie or a coffee house, and we weren't permitted in theaters and many places of entertainment. As a result, we spent more time at home as a family. Because my parents worked, during the week we ate dinner together in the kitchen, simple meals of boiled potatoes, cottage cheese, and vegetables. But Friday nights were special.

Before the eve of Shabbat, my mother worked in the kitchen preparing meals for the weekend while my father tidied up the apartment. The table, with a white cloth used only on Fridays, was set with tall, ornate silver candlesticks that she had inherited from her parents. A peaceful atmosphere prevailed as we stood together with my mother while she lit candles, held her hands up, and whispered the blessings. Then she gazed at the dazzling flame, and after a moment of silence, closed her eyes in contemplation. I often wondered what she was thinking then. I looked forward on Friday nights to fresh *Barchis* (challah), chicken soup and perhaps a pot roast or roast chicken. My favorite desserts were my mother's fruit compote or rice pudding or a baked apple.

On Friday nights we went to the Prinzregentenstrasse synagogue. In the temple, even when I was little, I felt something deep within me. The words, prayers, and the inspiring music with cantor and choir were all part of the experience, which calmed my spirit. When it came to the *Kiddush*, the sanctification of wine, the rabbi invited the children to participate. From the time I was six years old, I had memorized the words and melody of the *Kiddush* by listening to the cantor.

Jewish children were still allowed to play in public parks but permitted to sit only on benches labeled *Nur fuer Juden* (Only for Jews). To make us even more conspicuous, the benches were painted yellow. One hot summer day my high school girlfriend, Inge Wolf, and I walked to the nearby *Stadtpark* (city park) to join some classmates for a ball game. Suddenly a brown-shirted hoodlum with a swastika armband, obviously a member of the Hitler Youth, leaped out from behind a chestnut tree and threatened me with a knife.

"Dirty Jew," he yelled. *"Juden geht nach Palestina!* (Go to Palestine! Get out of Germany!)"

Perhaps feeling I had to prove myself and impress Inge, I lost my temper, not knowing what possessed me at that moment. Furious and impetuous, I punched him in the nose. It happened so fast, he didn't know what hit him.

"I'll get you by the balls, *Du Saujude* (Jewish pig)" he screamed, shaken by the sudden blow and the blood streaming from his nose.

Inge and I fled the scene as fast as our legs would carry us. Fortunately, the young thug did not follow us. It was the last time my feet ever traversed the *Stadtpark*. When I arrived home, out of breath, my mother immediately suspected something was wrong. As I reported both the incident and my irascible behavior following the assault, she became pale and frightened.

"Do you realize what you did?" Her voice shook as she reproached me. "You endangered our lives by your actions!"

Then I understood it was very risky of me to have taken such a chance. I should have known better. But the story doesn't end here. When I quoted to my mother the Nazi's remark regarding my genitalia, I became aware of a discrepancy. I was totally confused because I had only one testicle, while the Nazi used the plural word. Consequently, I had to submit to a rather embarrassing examination by my mother. She confirmed my finding.

Without delay we went to see Dr. Hahn, a Jewish doctor and surgeon. Upon examining me, he verified that I had a missing testicle and recommended surgery to correct the problem. The following week, I found myself recovering from a procedure to repair an undescended testicle. So the assault in the park was not a total loss.

Who could have predicted that the vitriolic remark of a Nazi hoodlum would send me to the hospital for an operation that I needed anyway?

*Chapter Six*

# Moving

Hitler's aim was to conquer the world. Within a few short years of taking control of Germany in 1933, he seemed to be making dramatic progress toward his goal, all the while continuing to blame Jews and Communists for Germany's defeat during World War I.

By the time I was twelve—in 1938—the already bad situation for the Jews was further deteriorating. I particularly remember the night in March when my father came home for dinner, holding the evening paper in his hand. We saw immediately that the news—the *Anschluss*—was grim. Hitler had annexed Austria without the slightest resistance from the Austrian people. In silence I stared at the newspaper photo showing Hitler's entrance into Vienna, leading a motorcade. Buildings were decorated with Nazi flags while cheering women held flower bouquets and ecstatically welcomed the new liberator.

Suddenly none of us was hungry. The food on the dining room table sat untouched, and an aura of despair descended over our home that night. Like other Jews, we finally saw the writing on the wall. Panic beset my parents. My father was a proud German, but he was also a naïve optimist, not taking seriously Hitler's slogan of "Today Germany and tomorrow the world." As a decorated Jewish war veteran, he never imagined how his dedication to the German cause would later be so brutally scorned. Up until the *Anschluss*, he believed Hitler would not last long and that Nazism would blow over. My mother, however, had always believed otherwise.

By July 1938 the desperation of Jews trying to escape the Nazis and their difficulty in obtaining immigration visas attracted such international attention that President Roosevelt convened a conference to address the problem. At Evian-les-Bain on the French shore of Lake Geneva, representatives from thirty-two countries attended including Europe, the United States, and Australia. Roosevelt sent his emissary, Myron Taylor, to chair the conference. The League of Nations' High Commissioner for Refugees also participated along with twenty representatives from various countries who formed a subcommittee to evaluate the plight of the Jews from Germany and Austria.

The outcome was disappointing. Most Jews had little faith in the conference from the start, pointing out that Evian spelled backwards is *naive*. Only a few countries allowed a tiny number of immigrants to their shores. Had the Conference been successful, perhaps the Holocaust might never have taken place. Hitler ridiculed Evian, proclaiming it as evidence that, "We do not want the Jews and no one else in the world wants them either."

Continuing his relentless tirade, Hitler decreed that documents of Jews be distinctively marked. On August 17, 1938 a law was passed requiring that each Jewish Kennkarte or identification card have a red "J" (for Jew) plus *Israel* added to males' family names and *Sara* for women's. On October 5, 1939 the Law on Passports was declared and my family was issued new documents that included the discriminatory additions.

In September 1938 Hitler decreed that the licenses of Germany's Jewish physicians and lawyers be revoked, and that Jewish businesses be ordered to display their owners' names on the store windows. The turning point, though, that marked the unmistakable beginning of the end for Jews took place on November 9, 1938—"The Night of Broken Glass."

Although this attack—*Kristallnacht*—had been meticulously planned for a long time, the Nazis used as a convenient pretext the murder of Ernst von Rath, a secretary at the Germany embassy in Paris. Rath was shot by Hershel Grynszpan, a young Jewish student whose Polish parents had been living in Silesia, Germany, but had not become German citizens. In his rage to rid Germany of its Jews, Hitler deported the Grynszpans along with 17,000 other Polish Jews who thus abruptly lost their Silesian homes and livelihoods. Grynszpan had intended to kill the German ambassador in retaliation for his parents' deportation.

On November 10, the day after *Kristallnacht*, I left home in the morning and walked undaunted as usual to my high school in the synagogue on *Prinzregentenstrasse*. On the way I was shocked to see Jewish-owned businesses ransacked, windows smashed and stores looted. With trepidation, I reached the synagogue school and to my horror found the building engulfed in flames. Our teacher, pale and frightened, met us in front.

"No school today, children. Go home quickly," she urged in a trembling voice.

Although the Berlin fire department stood by with their hoses, they made no attempt to put out the synagogue fire; they were concerned only about protecting the neighboring houses. I raced home, fearful and out of breath, bringing the shocking news to my parents even though I realized later that my mother already knew what had happened.

Soon we learned that during the *Kristallnacht* conflagration the Nazis had burned down and destroyed over one thousand synagogues and temples in Germany and Austria. The Gestapo arrested my Uncle Leo, who lived in Dresden, along with thirty thousand other Jews, and hauled them off to various concentration camps. To avoid arrest himself, my father felt he would be safer hiding in the home of Aunt Else, who lived on the other end of town. He was lucky. The Nazis did not come for him there.

Now it was clear—there was no hope for us. Hitler had spelled out his program, which left no doubt of his intentions.

"We must move!" my mother again insisted with absolute determination. But where could we go? Emigration was not easy. My parents were desperately trying to leave Germany, but the obstacles were formidable and most countries had strict immigration policies. Since 1921 U.S. immigration laws allowed an annual total of only 100,000 newcomers, a number not to exceed three percent of each country's population. The German quota was never filled because in pre-Hitler days German Jews were still comfortable and didn't intend to leave. Polish Jews, by contrast, were eager to immigrate to America because of prevalent anti-Semitism, so the three-percent Polish quota was quickly filled. In 1924 the U.S. Congress further reduced the annual number of immigrants to just two percent from each country.

Earlier, many Jews could have been saved but by the late 1930s the world closed its doors and the Jewish situation drastically worsened. More Jews lost their jobs, and many more were accosted and arrested. Desperate to get a visa, we stood for hours at the American Consulate along with hundreds of other distraught Jews. But it was hopeless. We might have applied for a number but one could wait for years if the number was, for example, 700, and only 200 people were given permission. Even if the U.S. immigration quotas weren't filled, there was another problem. Since the Great Depression, xenophobic attitudes prevailed in the U.S. and immigration was restricted or curtailed. Palestine was still eager to accept Jews to save them from Hitler, but Britain's quotas had closed that door too.

We ran from South American to the Canadian and Australian consulates. The lines were long, each day only a few visas were issued, and my parents' efforts were of no avail. Beside our passports, we had only a police clearance proving that we had no criminal record, but that was a relatively worthless piece of paper. Even if we had been lucky enough to possess an affidavit of sponsorship for a particular country, we would still have had to wait for a number.

Some individuals who were able to get their numbers moved up probably had not only sponsorship, but also specific skills that would be an asset to the country of sponsorship. Rabbis, for example, may have been needed in some community and certainly a scientist like Einstein would have had no problem emigrating. But my family had nothing. For us, Shanghai and Trinidad were among the few places in the world where Jews could go at that time.

Frantic, we chose China. With the price of a steamship ticket and some meager savings, we received permission to enter. I got out my atlas to locate this far-flung point in the Far East and learned that Shanghai used to be called "the Paris of the Orient." The flourishing business and cultural capital of China, Shanghai was a prosperous, international port city. It was also, at the same time, crime-ridden and filled with brothels, opium dens, and poor people. Nevertheless, China was our last resort. We had no other choice but to escape to the unknown.

My mother wanted to say goodbye to my elderly maternal grandmother, who lived in an old people's home in Breslau. We went together on the four-hour train trip. The visit was a crushing experience for my mother, who wept when she realized that her own mother was so senile she no longer recognized her own daughter.

In Berlin we began saying our goodbyes to Cecilia, my paternal grandmother, a widow who lived next door to us. Since my Bar Mitzvah was coming up the following spring, Cecilia presented me with a gift—a ring to mark my forthcoming passage into manhood. A beautiful gold signet, it originally was my grandfather's wedding band, which she had redesigned and engraved with my initials "HC." Unfortunately, my enjoyment of this gift was short-lived. According to the latest Nazi law, in order for non-Aryans to obtain clearance papers to leave Germany, they were required to turn over their valuables, including jewelry, gold and silver. So, shortly before our departure, two inspectors arrived at our apartment carrying a wooden barrel.

On the spot they confiscated priceless treasures that had been in our family for generations. Piece by piece, my parents set into the barrel our family silverware, our sterling silver trays and beautiful candelabras, including the candlesticks that had belonged to my great-grandparents, the sterling silver ones we used every Friday evening to welcome the Sabbath. Naturally, it was emotionally upsetting for my parents to part with these items, but we had no choice. Besides, they were only material objects and above all else we valued our lives more.

One German inspector, short and bald, wearing a swastika armband, watched every move we made. At one time he bent over to inventory the booty and stuck his head into the barrel. I thought he would almost fall in. It looked quite amusing to me and I bit my tongue to keep from laughing.

My father had a solid gold pocket watch that was a gift from his father. Painful as it was to give up, he pulled it out of his jewelry case, and it too helped fill the barrel.

"What about the wedding rings on our fingers?" Teary-eyed, my mother inquired.

"You can keep them if you like!" the short inspector replied with an abrupt smirk.

Unable to utter a word, I stood there motionless. I wanted very much to keep the signet ring in memory of my grandmother, but upon my mother's insistence, it too had to join the Nazis' loot. She feared keeping the ring might jeopardize our leaving Germany and her concern soon proved to be right.

With a heavy heart we put up a "Moving Sale" sign in front of the house and sold our furniture for a pittance. After purchasing tickets to Shanghai, we shipped a few boxes of clothes, books, and small household items. Then we packed our bags with only meager necessities. It was high time to say good-bye to our native land. I would not see Germany again until many years later.

# CHINA YEARS

## Chapter Seven

# Free at Last

On March 27, 1939 my parents and I departed Berlin by train with our packed suitcases and our per-person allowances of only ten German marks. The first stop on our journey to faraway Shanghai would be Munich and from there another train to Genoa. Leaving Berlin on a dismal, rainy morning made the prospect of sunny Italy even more desirable.

By evening we arrived, with some trepidation, at the birthplace of the Nazi movement—Munich—where anti-Semitism was still rife. Because we couldn't afford a hotel, we stayed overnight in the waiting hall of the train station, near the same Munich *Hofbrau Haus* where in 1923 Hitler first began his tirades against the Jews.

My very cautious mother, always planning ahead, had stuffed into her hand luggage a large beef salami, a loaf of bread, and a jar of mustard. In the station, permeated by the smells of beer and tobacco, we sat quietly munching our meager sandwiches and waiting anxiously for the night to end. Tense and frightened, my parents huddled in a corner while I dozed.

In the morning, the train for Genoa arrived exactly on schedule. Mounting the second-class car, we settled into our compartment, shared with a German couple on their way to a holiday in Italy. When the conductor blew the whistle, the steam locomotive began puffing and the train slowly left Munich. We breathed a sigh of cautious relief that soon Germany would be behind us.

In order not to attract attention, my parents and I spoke to each other in whispers. Although the passing Bavarian countryside was beautiful, we were much too nervous to look out the window and enjoy it. At the Brenner Pass, on the German-Italian border, the compartment door was suddenly thrown open and two storm troopers burst in.

"Inspection! Let's see your passports," they shouted.

My parents turned ashen and I was startled when they pulled me out to be strip-searched. The men frisked and fingered me all over my body, looking for jewelry and currency, but their suspicion was in vain. They found nothing because my mother had wisely urged me to give up my Bar Mitzvah ring before we left Berlin. The German couple observed this whole scene but did not utter a word.

The border police examined our passports, perhaps wanting to make sure that my mother's had the extra "Jewish" *Sarah* and my father's and mine had *Israel* added to our family name. I still have my old passport and although it is somewhat faded, its red "J" is still very clear. Our documents were worthless, but nevertheless the border police examined our photos, which still served as some form of identification. After they placed a stamp on our invalid papers, the train entered Italian territory and we officially left Germany, lost our citizenship and became stateless refugees. I would not set foot on German soil again for many, many years.

After another day and another night of travel, we arrived in Genoa hungry and exhausted but also elated. We had reached our goal! What was left of the salami sausage provided yet another meal for us. Although Genoa was bathed in brilliant morning sunshine, we had no time for sightseeing because our ship was leaving that same day.

Hurrying to the harbor, we excitedly boarded the *Conte Biancamano*, the huge ocean liner that would take us to Shanghai. Over 1,500 other Jewish refugees also boarded in Genoa. Like my family, they too had been robbed of homes, possessions, human dignity, and were no longer welcome in our German or Austrian homelands.

The ship stopped briefly in Naples while goods were loaded on, but we remained aboard. Then we entered the Mediterranean, heading for Port Said, the entrance to the Suez Canal. As third-class passengers, my parents and I had economy-class accommodations. We slept on bunk beds in an inside cabin and ate at long banquet tables, unlike the first-class travelers who had elegant rooms, dined at individual tables, and were catered to by service personnel.

The economy area had a no-frills play area and a limited library, where I passed the often monotonous days at sea by reading. I also joined other third-class playmates by adventurously sneaking into the first-class facility, which was well-equipped, to play ping-pong, shuffleboard, or to watch movies. When the weather was pleasant, my parents enjoyed sitting in deck chairs.

We had started our journey shortly before Passover, but the Italian liner had not anticipated the need to provide matzah, the unleavened bread Jews are commanded to eat during that eight-day holiday. Fortunately, the local Jewish community in Port Said, aware of our predicament, came to our aid and had cases of matzah delivered to our ship so we could observe Passover properly.

The shipboard Passover *Seder* (meal) was an unforgettable experience. Passover, whose theme is freedom from slavery, celebrates the Jewish people's exodus from Egypt four thousand years ago. That very first Seder took place when the Israelites crossed the Red Sea (Sea of Reeds) on their way to the Holy Land. By remarkable coincidence, our shipboard Seder took place as we sailed across the *same* Red Sea on the *exact date* of the holiday—April 14, 1939. It was a balmy night. No breeze disturbed the quiet of the evening, and the smooth water reflected a full moon and a starry sky. We Jews, fleeing Germany, were vicariously experiencing our own freedom from oppression—but our oppressors were Nazis instead of Egyptians.

I sat at the Seder table as a witness, listening to the story in German and also reading the Hebrew *Hagaddah* (the book explaining the Passover service). At least fifty children were aboard and since I wasn't the youngest, I didn't get to ask the traditional Four Questions. In the Orthodox Berlin day schools I had attended, I learned more than my father had ever been exposed to, so I was better able to keep up with the rituals, the Hebrew, and the Passover songs.

Unfortunately, the matzah we received in Port Said was indeed "the bread of affliction." Instead of the traditional dry, unleavened bread, it was damp and not very palatable, so a lot was left uneaten. The next day, in fact, we dumped large quantities into the sea to feed the fish. But the spirit of that Passover—with its inspirational message of freedom—still remains vivid in my memory even after all these years.

Our voyage continued via Aden, Bombay, Ceylon, Singapore, Manila, and Hong Kong. On the last leg of the journey, between Hong Kong and Shanghai, an evening storm broke out. A typhoon of enormous proportions lashed against the ship. Giant waves crashed onto the deck, tossing the ship mercilessly while rain came down in fierce torrents.

From the safety of the ocean liner, we watched in horror as two Chinese fishing boats capsized in the tumultuous waters. Anguished, we witnessed the doomed men desperately fighting for their lives. We stood by, helpless, as the ship's brave crew threw ropes and life rafts overboard, frantically trying to rescue the fishermen. It was hopeless. Exposed to the elements, the men disappeared, vanishing under huge waves. For the first time in my life, I encountered death and saw people drown. This dreadful picture too is still indelibly etched in my memory.

The following morning, after thirty long days at sea, we arrived in Shanghai—shaken, but thankful and ready to begin a new life.

## Chapter Eight

# A New Beginning

After nearly thirty days, the *Conte Biancamano* laid anchor in the harbor of Shanghai on April 29, 1939. At last we had made our way to China, the country that agreed to accept 20,000 stateless souls without visas carrying invalid passports.

Walking down the gangplank was like entering a new and unknown world. My parents and I were dazzled by the sights, sounds, and smells—all so startlingly different from anything I had ever encountered. The spring air that day was filled with a fishy odor commingled with the smoke emanating from chimneys of the many ships waiting to be unloaded. Fishing boats, flat-bottomed sampans, and water rickshaws interspersed with junks and their pole masts formed a colorful, lively silhouette along the imposing Wang Poo River.

Nearby, facing the harbor was the "Bund," Shanghai's most famous avenue, sometimes called the European Wall Street, lined with banks, hotels, and consulates. Amid the horrendous traffic, coolies carried their loads with antiphonal chants of *Heya! Hoya!* Hand-pulling their rickshaws alongside trucks, automobiles, and bicycles, they dodged beggars in tattered clothes, lying in the streets. I wondered if I would ever get used to this alien culture so unlike Europe, but I knew that only time would tell.

On the dock, a table was set up where a Jewish International Relief Committee welcomed us, registered us as stateless refugees, and distributed some kind of identification papers to use in China. Many newcomers were met by relatives who themselves had come a few months earlier. Those who could afford it moved anywhere in Shanghai and settled into a comfortable life. My family, like the majority of refugees, though, had no money and no idea where we would spend even the first night. Feeling apprehensive but also ready for whatever was next, we were loaded onto open trucks and driven to Hongkew, the poorest district of Shanghai.

Refugees were scattered among the various *Heime* (homes) facilities, which were converted out of the few remaining structures that survived the Sino-Japanese war (1937–39). Our first temporary residence was the Chaoufoong Road *Heim* originally owned by the London Mission Society. Several buildings were in fairly good condition, so they were made available as a dormitory, dining hall and clinic for the refugees. Giving up our privacy in shared housing was a new and uncomfortable experience for us. About fifty adults were accommodated in the 'community bedroom'—a large room resembling an army barracks with double bunks.

Our family was separated for the first time when I was moved to another building that housed children my age. After living there together in close quarters, I came down with scarlet fever, which started in the room to which I was assigned, and then became a minor epidemic. Consequently, a number of us were quarantined for ten days. Newcomers were arriving by the thousands, so some additional dormitories had to be established. After ten days in the *Heim* we were, fortunately, able to rent for ourselves a small one-room apartment. What a relief!

From the moment we arrived in Shanghai, it was mainly the Sassoon and Kadoorie families who extended a helping hand to us. Their philanthropy was boundless. For these magnanimous people, the concept of homeless Jews did not exist. Indigent refugees were housed in the Sassoon-owned Embankment Building or in heime shelters, converted dormitories and schools.

The Sassoons and Kadoories, Sephardi Jews, were British subjects from Baghdad who immigrated to Shanghai in 1845 as merchants, not refugees. Earlier, in Bombay, India, they had made their fortune first in cotton and then expanded their lucrative business to Shanghai. Widely known as the Rothschilds of the East, they were ardent Zionists and also observant Jews. In Shanghai they established a Jewish community, built a synagogue, kept the Jewish dietary laws, and closed their offices on the Sabbath and holidays.

Sir Victor Sassoon worked tirelessly to help the newcomers get settled. In the "soup kitchen," each person was guaranteed one hot meal a day, which sometimes included goulash soup, bread, and tea. I remember queuing up with an aluminum pan and an enamel cup. We sat on wooden benches and ate our simple fare at picnic tables. A relief committee at the school arranged for all students to have porridge for breakfast in the morning. Sometimes it was a little burnt and hard to get down, but we ate it gratefully. A "milk fund" was established for children to provide added nutrition.

Among the few bright spots in Hongkew was the magnificent school that Horace Kadoorie established for us. The majority of Jewish refugee children attended the Kadoorie School or SJYA (Shanghai Jewish Youth Association), which made it possible for everyone to receive a fine education. Mr. Kadoorie engaged an outstanding faculty who taught us English, French, and Hebrew along with music, art, and sports.

The Kadoorie School principal was Mrs. Lucie Hartwich, my former principal and teacher from Berlin. She was thrilled to have me reappear in Shanghai and I was delighted too because while attending her private school in Berlin, I developed a special relationship with her. In Shanghai, she also came to our class with her guitar and sang with us. Later, I would follow in her footsteps and take up the guitar when I became a cantor. Mr. Epstein, our music teacher, started a children's choir, which I joined. I also became one of the leaders who helped organize a weekly Shabbat service. Horace Kadoorie himself often attended and he would pass around candy at the end.

A special joy for me was the vocational club run by Professor and Mrs. Wilhelm Deman. In addition to ballroom dancing, we were taught etiquette—how to sit at the table and how to hold our forks and knives properly. We even had our own model savings bank and I was elected its first president. The boys had workshops in bookkeeping, radio construction, and typing, and Mrs. Deman offered the girls a course in cooking and housekeeping, a group I was tempted to join.

Being voracious for knowledge, I always had great respect for all my teachers but one in particular was very special. Miss Hannah Manasseh taught kindergarten, and she was the object of my first crush. Although I was only an eighth-grader, I fell deeply in love with her. She was twenty years old, had curly brown hair, beautiful dark eyes, and looked like a Sephardic Barbie doll with an olive complexion. I remember her lacy pink blouse and tight-fitting blue pleated skirt.

During recess I watched her as she kept an eye on the kindergarteners out on the lawn. When she passed me, I blushed. She was so lovely I had erotic dreams about her during the night. Like Roxanne in *Cyrano deBergerac*, though, Hannah didn't know how much I adored her. At the end of the year, she got married. For a while I was woefully in mourning. Of course I couldn't have known that ten years later, at the age of twenty-three, I myself would end up with another beautiful teacher, one I would marry. But I will never forget Miss Manasseh, my first love.

It was other dedicated teachers, though, like Lucie Hartwich, Leo Epstein, and Leo Mayer who motivated me to later become an educator and a cantor.

# Chapter Nine

# Life in Hongkew

Poverty was a major problem among most of the refugees, or "displaced persons" as we were called. Many were well educated, but arrived totally penniless because the Nazis had stolen their possessions. Unable to speak Chinese, they depended on welfare, eking out a meager existence by doing manual labor. The Russian Jews who had arrived earlier, after the 1917 revolution, were much better off and were fairly well established. They helped the incoming refugees by opening soup kitchens under the auspices of HIAS, the Hebrew Immigrant Aid Society.

Times were tough for my family too, but my parents borrowed money so we moved and opened a little restaurant. We lived upstairs in a small apartment with two rooms and a WC (toilet), which was a luxury. For the restaurant we improvised window curtains, covered the concrete floor with linoleum, and put up a screen door to keep out the flies. At the restaurant entrance we placed a hand-painted sign in German, announcing the specials of the day.

We could seat twenty people or rearrange our modest wooden tables and chairs to accommodate small parties. Our patrons were primarily Austrian and German refugees, but occasionally we had visits from foreign officials in charge of the International Settlement. One German inspector who worked for the Health Department particularly enjoyed our European-style cuisine.

My mother was a wonderful homemaker and a superb cook. She labored hard in the kitchen preparing tasty meals without ever using a cookbook, following a recipe, or even measuring ingredients. It was always a handful of this and a handful of that with a pinch of salt and pepper added to taste.

One of her specialties was *Sauerbraten* (marinated beef) with potato pancakes. To produce such a dish was quite an art itself, considering that the

31

primitive stoves in the kitchen were fueled with charcoal, a popular fuel readily available at local markets. We needed to constantly add charcoal and use a hand-operated fan to increase the flames, which released carbon monoxide and soot. Even though we kept the kitchen window open, we couldn't help inhaling the noxious fumes. No wonder so many people suffered respiratory-related illnesses in China.

My family worked together in the restaurant. While my mother was expert at cooking, my father, a former salesman, was inexperienced at waiting on tables and so was somewhat clumsy. After school I helped in the kitchen by washing dishes, peeling potatoes, and cleaning vegetables. In those days, deliveries were rare, so my parents had to get up very early in the morning to buy meat and produce at the nearby open air market. Sometimes I came along and with my good memory and musical ear, I used my increasing knowledge of street Chinese to help bargain for a good price.

Coming from Germany, a country excessively concerned about cleanliness, my parents and I found Hongkew's sanitary conditions appalling, both inside and out. Our decrepit apartment was inhabited by numerous cockroaches, wandering around as if they owned the place. In the summer, lice caused typhus and mosquitoes bred malaria. All year round, countless people including refugees died of cholera, small pox, typhoid fever, tapeworm, and tuberculosis.

Because of the deplorable hygienic conditions, extreme care had to be taken with fruits and vegetables, since the common agricultural fertilizer came from human waste. Careful washing and thorough cooking were essential. Tap water —when available—was not safe to drink.

"Whatever you do, make sure to boil the water—even when brushing your teeth," the doctors warned.

Boiled water was available from Chinese hot water shops, located everywhere, within walking distance. Instead of using coins, the customer purchased little bamboo sticks and used them as tokens to buy a quart of boiling water, ladled out of kettles. Most people took their water away in a thermos to keep for tea or other purposes.

We were all extremely careful to drink only boiled water, yet our family's new life and new routine was abruptly and tragically altered just five months after we arrived in Shanghai. My mother—slaving away in our restaurant, cooking over a hot stove twelve hours a day, seven days a week—accidentally consumed some contaminated water and died of amoebic dysentery at the age of fifty-three. Penicillin did not yet exist so she was given injections of Emetine Hydrochloride, which did not help.

Although a hospital had opened to care for sick refugees, Jewish doctors had not yet learned how to handle subtropical diseases like cholera, typhoid, malaria, and amoebic dysentery. My mother was among the first to succumb.

Later, when my father also became ill from amoebic dysentery, I took him to a local Chinese hospital, where he was treated by Chinese doctors familiar with such diseases; they often prescribed plain rice water as a cure.

My mother's death left my father and me devastated, but I felt it was my job to comfort him because he didn't think he could survive being alone without her.

"Dad," I tried to console him, "you still have me to be with you."

But I wasn't very successful. My relationship with my father was good, but unfortunately he never gave me the inner support I so badly needed after losing my mother, especially since I was just thirteen. Although he was always proud of me, he never uttered the words I most yearned to hear—*my son, I love you*. His reticence often made me feel inadequate, so I knew I would have to find my own way in the world and learn to take risks.

Together my father and I had laid my mother to rest in the Russian Jewish cemetery on Baikal Road. Since we were short on finances, we arranged for a modest funeral and a few friends joined us at the graveside service. On her freshly dug grave, we placed in the ground a little marker with the inscription: Ida Cohn, nee Graupner, 1886–1939.

Shortly after my mother's death, I contracted yellow jaundice, a liver disorder similar to a mild case of hepatitis, an ailment that to this day has left me ineligible to donate blood. For three weeks I was very sick. My skin and even my eyes turned yellow from the disease. Grieving over the loss of my mother, feeling isolated and ill, I stayed in bed in our miserable little apartment. The doctor suggested the jaundice might have been caused, or at least exacerbated by, my emotional distress at losing my mother.

In September 1939, the month of my mother's funeral, Hitler invaded Poland and World War II began. By then, we learned that immigration to Shanghai was closed. Had our family remained only a few more months in Berlin, we would have met the same fate as those Jews who remained in Germany and perished in the concentration camps.

## Chapter Ten

# My Bar Mitzvah

"Today I am a Man" is a famous sentence sometimes spoken by a 13-year-old Jewish boy when he delivers his Bar Mitzvah speech during the synagogue ceremony. These words, of course, were never meant in the literal sense, but they do signify that at thirteen, a Jewish male attains the age of religious majority. In my case, however, the expression "Today I am a Man" had real meaning because by the time I had my Bar Mitzvah (which literally means Son of the Commandment), I was almost fourteen and had indeed become a man after working for nearly a year to support myself.

Had my family stayed in Germany, I would have had my Bar Mitzvah in Berlin at the customary age. But we arrived in Shanghai in April 1939, a month before my thirteenth birthday, and we were overwhelmed—still feeling the tension and anxiety of leaving Germany while struggling to adapt to our new Chinese homeland, and trying to open a restaurant so we could earn a living. I certainly was not prepared to become a Bar Mitzvah, so my parents and I agreed to postpone that occasion for one year. That decision proved to be wise especially after my mother died.

I dropped out of the excellent Kadoorie School in order to help my father keep our restaurant in business. My favorite teacher, Lucie Hartwich, was disappointed that I had to interrupt my education. Even though I was not a model student, she had a warm spot in her heart for me and she was full of compassion after my mother's death.

By the time I was fourteen my unanticipated culinary career was well underway. I started as a dishwasher, advanced to a potato peeler, and finally became a full cook, learning how to prepare European-style food. Often I worked ten hours a day, seven days a week, perspiring behind a hot stove with an open fire, inhaling smoke from the burning coals. It's a small wonder I didn't come down with some lung disease.

My father hired Frau Wasserberg to be our new Jewish cook. I learned so much about German and Viennese dishes from this talented lady that when she got sick at times, I was able to take over to keep the place going.

"Do you have a new cook, Mr. Cohn?" some guests would inquire after sampling my Hungarian Goulash.

"Oh no," my father would answer. "My son is in charge today."

"The Goulash was especially tasty today. I hope your cook is sick more often," guests would reply.

My father was proud of me and so were our Chinese assistants, who helped me learn more Chinese and often praised me in Pidgin English, "Han Su (Hans), you vely nicee, vely clever boy."

In addition to working with my father at the restaurant, each day I got up early to fulfill the Jewish tradition of reciting *Kaddish*, the mourner's prayer in memory of a deceased parent. Although I wasn't Orthodox, I wanted to follow this eleven-month practice to honor my mother's memory. Nearby, a makeshift synagogue — rebuilt and converted from a bombed-out building — conducted regular Sabbath services and a daily Minyan, a service requiring at least ten male worshippers.

During the year of mourning, I became so familiar with the Hebrew prayers I could almost recite them by rote, but I had no idea what I was saying. Some of the older men rattled off their prayers at a tremendous speed, and I tried to keep up with them but it was a lost cause. Slowly, I also learned the melodies by diligently listening to Cantor Fleischer, the presiding leader. Many years later I would eventually understand both the Hebrew and the liturgy.

The local Jewish community arranged for me to receive a weekly tutoring lesson for Bar Mitzvah from Cantor Fleischer, who was young but not very patient. He insisted on standing close to me and barked each tune into my ear. By the time I got home, the melody escaped me completely. Because I was busy working at the restaurant, I usually got around to practice only on the day of the lesson. By then I'd forgotten not only the tune, but also everything else I had learned at the previous session.

"What have you been doing all week? Why didn't you practice?" Cantor Fleischer would yell. "Did you come here to waste my time?"

He was so angry and close to hitting me. Finally it dawned on me, that if, immediately after the lesson, I hummed the new tune while walking home, I could solve the problem. So I chanted away in Hebrew, reinforcing the melodies in my memory. Years later the tape recorder was invented. I wish I'd had one back then.

In preparation for the Bar Mitzvah, my father purchased a secondhand navy blue suit for me. We took it to Mr. Klein, a kindhearted tailor who said, "We'll fix you up, my boy! You'll look great when I'm done." Then he measured me, took the whole garment apart, and proceeded to turn it inside out so the less worn sections were on the outside. He performed a miracle. When the day arrived, I wore the reconstituted suit with a white shirt, new tie, and new shoes. I looked like a fashion model.

The Bar Mitzvah took place near Purim on March 19, 1940 at Hongkew's Ohel Moshe (the Tent of Moses) synagogue on Ward Road. This Russian-Jewish orthodox *Shul* was built in the Eastern European style with men seated downstairs and women in the upstairs gallery. Jokingly the men would say, "Here, we look up to our ladies!"

The synagogue was filled with many of my friends and I was the center of attention. Blessed with a fine voice, I sang like a bird, my portions were from both the Torah (*Pentateuch*) and the Haftorah (Prophets) for *Shabbat VaYikra*. The people loved it. After I finished chanting the rabbi gave his sermon, adding, "If only your mother could have heard you today, she would have been so proud. But we know she is here with us in spirit. Her love for you will never die." At that, the women seated above felt even sorrier for the poor kid whose mother had died seven months earlier and heavy sobbing was heard from the gallery.

For my Bar Mitzvah party, I invited ten of my closest school friends to a special dinner in my honor. My father engaged Frau Wasserberg, our restaurant cook, to prepare my favorite dish—*Wiener Schnitzel* with a fried egg on top. *Streussel Kuchen* was the dessert with apple cider as the beverage. As gifts I received three fountain pens, several books, and some new clothes. My Bar Mitzvah was a small event compared to today's standards, but it was very special for me. The spirit of that occasion set an emotional tone which would influence me to embark on career that would combine both my religious experience and my love of music.

A year after my mother's death it was time for the tradition of putting up a tombstone, to show that the deceased had not been forgotten. Often during the previous months I had gone to the nearby Baikal Road cemetery to visit her grave, murmuring a brief prayer in her memory and shedding a few tears. Standing by myself, surrounded by many carved stones in honor of those whom death had taken, I glanced at the small marker that bore my mother's name. It was tiny because we were too poor to erect a fitting monument for her.

Suddenly an idea came to mind. I decided to search among the Hongkew ruins for a rock that could be transformed, at little cost, into a tombstone. The area at that time still had no shortage of bombed-out houses, and as luck had it, I came across a rock that suited my needs. Borrowing a handcart and perspiring in the summer heat, I lugged my newly found treasure to a Chinese stonemason. The good man agreed for a small sum to carve the stone, engrave it with my mother's name, and mount it onto the grave.

There amidst the more impressive monuments in the cemetery stood my mother's stone—an unobtrusive remembrance of a quiet, modest, dignified woman. The monument, a sign to celebrate her life, was also a symbol of comfort to me.

## Chapter Eleven

# City of a Thousand Faces

Living in Shanghai was a fascinating eye-opener for me.

Curious about its history, I learned that in Chinese the word *Shanghai* means *up from the sea* and indeed the city was largely built up from the alluvial deposits of the China Sea. A thousand years ago these deposits, containing mud and silt, constituted a large swampland that created Shanghai as an insignificant fishing village.

At the end of the Opium War in 1842, China was defeated by the British, who declared Shanghai to be an "open" port, meaning it had no military value so was not subject to attack by an enemy. But during the Sino-Japanese War (1937–1939) the Chinese had fought fiercely before being defeated by Japan, which then occupied Manchuria, the greater part of North China, and the outskirts of Shanghai including Hongkew.

By 1939, when my family came to Shanghai, it was the second largest city in the world and the biggest city in the Asian continent with a population of five million. It was also an international trading center, attracting an incredible variety of people from the wealthiest in society to the lowest element found anywhere.

Shanghai was then divided into two separate but adjacent districts—the French Concession (or Frenchtown) and the International Settlement. The French Concession was exclusively patterned after French schools and government offices and the French language was spoken. The International Settlement, unofficially administered by the British, had its own police force and included sections representing America, Germany, and other European nations. The International Settlement was located by the shores of the Whangpoo (Yellow) River, and maintained a deep-water harbor not far from the Yangtze, which enters the China Sea.

My father and I lived on the border of the International Settlement in Hongkew, the poorest area and a rubble-torn remnant of its former condition. When the Sino-Japanese War ended, the International Settlement and the French Concession were unscathed but Hongkew's bombed-out buildings still resembled the ancient ruins of Athens. It was the arriving Jewish refugees who later would help begin to rebuild it.

In Shanghai every day one could witness amazing, shocking scenes that typified the deplorable conditions and terrible contrasts between wealth and poverty. The Chinese who lived among us in Hongkew suffered equally as much as we did. There seemed to be no real middle class. In winter it was not unusual to see people dying or to find corpses lying in the middle of the street, frozen to death. Passers-by would carefully walk around the dead, not daring to touch them for fear of being held responsible to pay for the funerals. Next to scenes like these, chauffeur-driven limousines frequented the boulevards while luxury hotels, furnished in the finest decor, catered to an international clientele. Department stores carried the finest silks and most expensive jewelry.

Shanghai was notoriously corrupt and crime-infested. The most respectable judges could be bribed by criminals to obtain their freedom or be given a lesser sentence for a serious offense. Bribery was commonplace not only among lawyers but also among policemen on the street corner. Nightclubs and bars usually kept their doors open until the early morning hours. Casinos thrived seven days a week and millions of dollars changed hands throughout the night. Gambling houses prospered and prostitution was rampant.

People of all nationalities could be found in Shanghai. Anyone could enter the city without a passport or visa and then disappear without ever being detected. To be *shanghaied* became a nautical term referring to a sailor who was kidnapped or forced to join a ship's crew after getting drunk or being drugged by unscrupulous agents. Merchant marine and passenger ships docked by the hundreds and sailors from Sweden, Germany, Japan, Scandinavia, Italy and other international ports spilled onto the streets. They had a marvelous time spending their money on prostitutes and often in return took home venereal disease.

Some 1,500 opium dens located along the city's shopping areas were open to the public and did a booming business. Anyone passing by could detect the sweet smell of opium blending with the fragrance of incense candles, whose scents filled the air along with a potpourri of sounds. In the streets, Chinese music intermingled with highly popular American jazz and songs, especially those of Bing Crosby, a favorite. In movie houses showing American films, Roy Rogers was the most beloved hero. Maestro Mario Paci, an Italian, conducted Shanghai's wonderful symphony orchestra.

In international Shanghai, Western discrimination was frequently apparent. The elegant racetrack on the famous Bubbling Well Road posted a sign reading "Chinese and Dogs not permitted." While riding rickshaws, Scotchmen of the British Highlanders regiment wore traditional kilts, yelled "Chop, Chop," and sometimes used their sticks like riding crops, hitting the coolies as though they were horses.

By contrast, religious life thrived. Shanghai's spiritual side was reflected in beautiful pagodas, churches and synagogues. Drums and prayer wheels accompanied the mystical chanting in Buddhist temples, which were found everywhere. Church music was popular and missionaries actively proselytized to save Chinese souls.

A new element of culture was brought to Shanghai by the German and Austrian Jewish refugees who arrived in 1939. Little orchestras sprang up and Viennese waltzes were heard in coffee houses and bars, creating among us stateless Jews a nostalgic yearning for the homeland left behind. Jewish comedians entertained and for a short time laughter made people forget their troubles. Many refugees worked as musicians, waiters, nurses, and clerks in export houses.

My musical ear and a love for languages helped me continue to improve my Chinese, mainly from listening to people in the street. After a while I became fluent enough to act as an interpreter. Dr. Glaser, a German-Jewish physician proficient at treating venereal diseases, hired me to translate for his Chinese patients. I came to his office two afternoons a week, and he paid me ten percent of his fee.

Dr. Glaser's patients were not pleasant to look at, but I soon learned the Chinese medical terms for their conditions: syphilis, gonorrhea, emissions, blisters, pus, and rash. Dr. Glaser treated most cases in a similar way, and I particularly remember the injections he used—Salvarsan (*Lo-Ling-Lo* 606), a substance invented by Dr. Paul Ehrlich, a German Jew who discovered a cure for syphilis. It was only after 606 tries to remedy the dreaded disease that Ehrlich came up with a cure that eventually won him the Nobel Prize in 1908.

By 1941 after struggling for a year to keep our restaurant going, my father sold it, finding the effort too difficult to continue without his wife. Instead, he located work as a watchman and I, in addition to translating for Dr. Glaser, became a cook in a European-style restaurant with a bakery. The bakery's specialty was *Salzstangen*, a breadstick sprinkled with salt. I arranged with the owner's brother, the baker, to purchase at cost about thirty *salzstangen*, and after work I packed the pastries in a breadbasket and went out to sell them to people leaving a nearby movie theater.

The small profit I made helped a lot because the restaurant pay was so low. Although the smoky air around the hot ovens never agreed with my voice, my minimal earnings were hardly enough to pay for the singing lessons I took with Mr. Kalischer, a Jewish musician and voice teacher. When he introduced me to Schubert *Lieder*, a whole new world opened up for me.

In the meantime, though, I further improved my culinary and pastry skills. I seemed to have the right touch as well as an active imagination, and I often thought of my mother as I prepared outstanding dishes, wondering if I had inherited her gift for cooking. I too had an intuitive sense of how to prepare and combine foods without following a recipe.

The cooking talent I developed in the slums of Shanghai helped my father and me to survive the bitter war years that were just ahead. Shanghai was neither hell nor paradise, but it was where I learned to swim, to hold my head above water to keep from drowning. For me, Shanghai was a place of survival. While many others suffered and died from malnutrition, my father and I were fortunate to have something to eat. I was able to negotiate with the restaurant where I worked to bring him a hot meal every day after work. Often he would wait up for me and eat at midnight.

Food was precious, but so was water—even the water that food was cooked in, such as the mashed potatoes I regularly made at one of Shanghai's European restaurants. I can never forget a fellow refugee, Kurt Langer, who would come to the back door of the kitchen asking for leftover water. Formerly a successful attorney in Germany, he appeared with a stubbly unshaven face, and a shabby, dilapidated suit that hung down from his underfed body.

*"Herr Cohn, haben Sie etwas warmes Kartoffelwasser fuer mich?"* he would ask. (Mr. Cohn, do you have some warm potato water for me?)

His voice quivered as he held out a wide-mouthed thermos and warmed his chilled body by devouring the hot liquid, which had some small nutritional value. When the boss wasn't looking, I occasionally sneaked in a few potatoes. That made his day. Mr. Langer was a faithful customer who came to see me often.

Sixty-three years have passed since then and I don't know whether Kurt Langer survived the war years in Shanghai. Yet, I can still see him looking into the kitchen window. To this day, when I cook potatoes, I think of him and I don't have the heart to dump this precious liquid into my kitchen sink. I carefully store it in the refrigerator and use it whenever I cook my favorite soups.

## Chapter Twelve

# A Subtle Hint

A black cloud settled over the Jewish community in Shanghai after Japan's catastrophic bombardment of Pearl Harbor in December 1941. Our already harsh life became even worse after America declared war on Japan. Disease and starvation were epidemic, and we faced one difficulty after another. Yet, we still considered ourselves fortunate to have escaped the Nazi horrors. From the few reports we received, it seemed clear that Jews in Europe were doomed.

The Japanese supported Germany. In September 1940 they had signed the Tripartite Axis Pact, a Berlin-Tokyo-Rome alliance. Although the Japanese were not particularly sympathetic to Jews, they generally treated us in a friendly, humane way. That all changed, however, after Heinrich Himmler, Hitler's Gestapo Chief, and Herman Goering, the most prominent Nazi next to Hitler, requested a conference at Wannsee to establish *a solution to the Jewish problem.* On January 20, 1942 the brief Wannsee meeting was chaired by Reinhard Heydrich, Chief of the Reich Security Office, and attended by the infamous Adolf Eichman and other leading Nazi officials. There the "Final Solution" was formulated—a plan to totally destroy world Jewry.

Until 1942, the Nazis had concentrated on deporting Jews only from German-occupied communities and sending them to death camps. After Wannsee, that approach greatly expanded beginning with Italy, a partner of the Third Reich, when Hitler ordered Mussolini to turn over his Jewish population.

Next, Hitler directed his attention to the Far East, demanding that his Japanese Axis partner follow Italy's example. When the Nazi government cast its eye on the Shanghai Ghetto and its 20,000 Jews, our destiny took yet another turn. To carry out Hitler's plan, Colonel Joseph Meisinger, Gestapo Chief in Warsaw, was transferred to Japan to be in charge of German affairs.

Meisinger, a notorious murderer known as the "Butcher of Warsaw," came to Tokyo intent on carrying out the Nazi policy that was established at Wannsee.

"Jews are not trustworthy," he insisted to the Japanese. "They support the allies." Hinting thus that Shanghai's Jewish community of 20,000 was a threat to the war effort, Meisinger made several proposals to resolve the "Jewish problem." His plans, however, fell on deaf ears because anti-Semitism did not exist then in Japan. Nevertheless, Meisinger was determined to entice the Japanese occupation authorities to liquidate the ghetto. In the spring of 1942 he boarded a Japanese submarine and made his way to Shanghai, along with Nazi colleagues Adolf Putkammer and Hans Neumann. Meisinger carried with him a supply of Zyklon-B gas, the deadly cyanide poison in the form of pellets, which the SS used so effectively, primarily at the Auschwitz death camp.

What Meisinger had earlier introduced in Tokyo as a subtle hint became a deadly serious recommendation in Shanghai, where he addressed a group of Japanese officials including Tsutomo Kubota, the Japanese naval officer in charge of Jewish affairs, Mitsugi Shibata, vice consul of the local consulate, and the Kempeitai (Japanese secret police).

Repeating his accusation that Shanghai Jews were traitors and saboteurs, Meisinger explained that Jews would be easy to round up on a holiday like Rosh Hashanah, the Jewish New Year, when the majority would be found in the synagogue. He enthusiastically presented three carefully calculated proposals.

The first plan, he said, was to bring the Jews to old, decrepit ships anchored in Pootung, across the Whangpoo River from Shanghai. Then, these boats would be towed out to the ocean and their cables cut. Left to their own devices and drifting aimlessly, the Jews would eventually starve to death. To hide the dead Jews' mortal remains, the ships would be torpedoed.

Meisinger's second proposal was to transport the rounded-up Jews up the Yangtze River to the island of Tzungming. There they would be forced to work in the salt mines as slaves, producing salt for Japan. Through hard labor and lack of food, their demise would not take long. In case the two previous ideas weren't acceptable, Meisinger proposed a third: Establish a concentration camp and exterminate the Jews with poison, as was being done in Auschwitz.

The Japanese officials were aghast, appalled at such proposals. Admittedly, they were war partners with Germany, but they declared they would never stoop so low as to even consider Meisinger's plans. Mitsugi Shibata, who had attended Meisinger's meeting with the Japanese, had many Jewish friends, so he appealed to the Tokyo authorities on behalf of the Shanghai Jews. Unfortunately, Meisinger's Shanghai meeting was leaked to the Jews. Shibata and

Kubota were blamed and arrested by the Shanghai *Kempeitai*, a ruthless branch of the Japanese military forces. Both men were punished, demoted, and sent back to Japan, but at least Meisinger's plans were foiled.

Although the Japanese authorities rejected Meisinger's Nazi solutions, they did offer their German partners a compromise. On February 18, 1943 Japan agreed to imprison Americans and British in camps and require all stateless European Jews to be settled in a ghetto, a designated area within Hongkew. As a result, Jews who lived in the International Settlement had to move into Hongkew, which was still a decrepit, poverty-stricken and war-damaged district.

Special passes were needed to leave the ghetto. Kanoh Goya, a Japanese appointed official was put in charge to issue special permission to those who were eligible to leave the ghetto on a daily basis. Among them were doctors and persons with permanent jobs who worked on the outside.

Goya, a short, moody individual with a terrible temper, made the decisions alone. At times, he could be friendly or cruel. He would scream or slap refugees at random. In a fit of rage he would stand on his desk and insult applicants and threw some of them out of his office. He had delusions of grandeur, saying with conviction, "I am the King of the Jews."

As we languished in the ghetto, a rumor began to circulate that Jews were to be transferred to the interior of China, but we didn't know why. At first this possibility sounded like welcome relief from the constant American air raids targeting military installations, which the Japanese had strategically placed near the Hongkew ghetto. The rumor, we learned only after the war, was true. Indeed, poison was found later in Shanghai storage houses ascribed to Bayer Pharmaceuticals and Siemens Chemical Corporation.

In the ghetto, our movements were restricted to an area of forty square blocks, under the supervision of Japanese authorities. Jewish volunteer police, called Pao Chia, wore armbands and were stationed near the ghetto boundaries to check the identification of everyone who had permits to work outside. My father, then employed as a watchman, had a special permit. Since at times I also had a job outside the ghetto, I had to show the police my pass, which was like the equivalent of a driver's license today.

Ordered to live in virtual confinement, our physical situation deteriorated quickly. Poor refugees like my family, who had been forced to leave everything behind in Germany, had moved into Hongkew from the very beginning. But other Jews, more fortunate than my father and me, were not considered stateless—those who came to Shanghai prior to Kristallnacht, those who could afford to live anywhere in the city, and Russian Jews, who were considered Soviet citizens. Russia was not viewed by Japan as an enemy until the summer of 1945 when it joined in the war against Japan.

Conditions in Hongkew were terrible. From one crisis to another, hardship was the order of the day. Yet almost ninety percent of us survived. Had Meisinger's barbaric plans been realized, though, I certainly would not be here today.

The Chinese have two symbols for the word *crisis*. One symbol denotes danger and fear, which we experienced daily, while the other represents hope. Even though living in this jungle deprived me of a happy youth, I managed to find hope and inner strength in prayer and music. There is a lesson in suffering, and in spite of an unhealthy environment, the School of Life taught me to discover my own identity, to value life, and especially to appreciate it while I had it.

*Chapter Thirteen*

# The Air Raid

In May of 1945 our community rejoiced twice. On May 7 we learned from the Russian Radio Station XMHA that Germany had surrendered unconditionally at the headquarters of General Eisenhower, Supreme Commander of the Allied Forces in Europe. On May 8 another surrender took place under the Soviets, who had occupied Berlin. Hitler had already committed suicide in a Berlin bunker and the war with Germany was at an end.

Although this news was wonderful, we in Hongkew were still under Japanese occupation and still kept in the Hongkew ghetto. For almost every day of the previous year, we endured blackouts as the U.S. Air Force, coming from Iwo Jima, bombed installations in Shanghai. The sound of those air raid sirens has haunted me ever since. Even today the wailing of police or ambulance sirens reminds me again of the fright I felt as those American B-17s flew low to reach their Japanese naval targets. I was terrified when the sirens shrieked and anti-aircraft fire lit up the skies along the Shanghai waterfront.

In the Hongkew ghetto we lived in substandard houses that had no air raid shelters. In fact, it was nearly impossible even to dig bomb shelters because most homes were built on land that was below sea level. Witnessing this situation, I understood what I had previously only read about—that the word *Shanghai* in Chinese actually does mean *up from the sea*.

During air raids, we sat in the dark and waited until the all-clear sounded. Usually bombs fell in the distance, so nothing happened in our immediate area. But the unexpected did take place on Tuesday, July 17, 1945. The U.S. Air Force intended to knock out a Japanese military radio station located near our ghetto, but the planes missed. Instead, the unintended target became the ghetto itself. We were accustomed to night raids, but this was the first attack in the idle of the day. Sirens wailed as dozens of B-29 bombers overhead in the blue sky released their deadly cargo, causing death and destruction in Hongkew.

When the tragedy occurred, I was working at Rosenberg's Restaurant and we were just serving lunch. Standing by the stove in the kitchen, which was located on the mezzanine floor, I was busy filling orders when Mr. Rosenberg, the owner, called me. I left the kitchen and came downstairs to get instructions from him.

Suddenly bombs fell all around us. A direct hit was followed by an explosion that struck the building next door to us. The walls were shaking and debris was flying. People were screaming, moaning in agony, taking shelter under the tables. I was flung to the floor and discovered shrapnel in my hand. It all happened so fast we hardly knew what hit us. Two minutes later it was over. I returned to the kitchen and looked for Tom the cat, my constant companion, who always stayed with me near the stove. He was shredded to bits. Luckily, I had been called downstairs or the same destiny would have awaited me.

While I was lucky to have escaped death, thirty-one of our people were killed including Dr. Felix Kardegg, the president of the Jewish community, as well as many more Chinese who lived among us. The Japanese authorities were helpful, sending ambulances and medical personnel to take the many injured to the hospital.

The next day, accompanying the deceased to the cemetery, we walked behind trucks that carried the dead. In the scorching summer heat, a mass funeral took place. The stench of human remains was so unbearable we had to cover our noses with handkerchiefs. Perspiration mingled with salty tears running down our faces.

The silent march of the mourners, along with the memorial prayers chanted by the cantor is another image that still lingers with me.

## Chapter Fourteen

# The Worst Thing I Ever Did

The American air raids continued relentlessly, but in the summer of 1945 the U.S. Air Force helped to end the war by dropping the atomic bomb.

On August 6 a B-29 bomber dropped "Little Boy" on Hiroshima, killing 70,000 persons. On August 9 a second bomb called "Fat Man" destroyed the city of Nagasaki, killing another 32,000. Two weeks later Emperor Hirohito went on the air to capitulate unconditionally.

On September 2, 1945 at 10:30 A.M. Japan's surrender took place at Tokyo Bay aboard the U.S. Battleship *Missouri*. After General Douglas MacArthur signed for the Allied Powers and Admiral Chester Nimitz for the United States, President Harry Truman officially proclaimed "V.J." Day.

The war was finally over and shouts of joy rang through the ghetto. Shalom! Shalom, the war is over! Peace is here! It was so much like a dream it didn't seem real. It was only later that we heard about the atomic bombs. Some time afterward we also learned that the U.S. had planned an August 15 air raid on Shanghai's Municipal Jail, which contained a munitions dump. The jail, located on Ward Road in the Hongkew ghetto, covered two city blocks. The air raid was cancelled after the atomic bomb was dropped. Had the raid actually taken place, though, it would have killed thousands of innocent Jews and Chinese. As sad and strange as it seems, the atomic bomb saved our lives.

When the war ended, of course we were happy, but the tragedies and atrocities that European Jews suffered had a deep and sobering effect on our gratefulness at being alive and free. While the war was raging, all communications with our European relatives were cut off, so we had no idea about the extent of Hitler's terror. We had heard of concentration or work camps but never of Auschwitz or other death camps. Only after 1945 did we learn what really happened, that millions of Jews were murdered.

The Red Cross published lists of both survivors and also those who perished. Some people were overjoyed to find their relatives' names, but many more were devastated to discover their loved ones had been murdered. Some, in fact, were so distraught they committed suicide after realizing they had no one left. My father and I were grief-stricken to know that most of our relatives had perished—five of my mother's six sisters and several cousins as well as Cecilia, my mother's mother, and Aunt Sophie, my father's sister.

After Japan was defeated, the Americans returned to Manila and Singapore and brought Chinese workers back to Shanghai, which once again became a major center for trade. The U.S. Army replaced the Japanese occupation forces and the U.S. Air Transport Command sent military planes to take over the Shanghai airport. Since I could speak Chinese, my language talent was in demand and I was hired as a civilian employee, assigned to help the American forces as an interpreter at the airport. I was just nineteen years old and thrilled to have such an opportunity.

My duty was to assist the supervising officer, Major White, who administered a warehouse that stored radio parts for replacement on planes. Having no similar prior experience, everything was new to me, and at first I was given minor responsibilities. I had never finished high school because my education was interrupted, but I was eager to please and highly motivated. These qualities contributed to my ability to quickly learn the skills needed.

From the beginning Major White took a liking to me and helped me in many ways. He taught me the names of various items like headsets, speakers, transmitters, microphones, and other supplies. He also trained me to keep an inventory of pieces such as tubes and various mechanical or electronic parts. I filled requisitions for pilots who ordered certain pieces, retrieved the items from the warehouse, and had them sent to the planes. I also translated English instructions for the Chinese workers, the civilian handymen who transported boxes, moved equipment, and performed other needed tasks.

Major White noticed that I had a youthful, tenacious spirit and an insatiable desire to accumulate knowledge. After a while in my new job, I felt confident enough to suggest some creative ideas that could be implemented at the warehouse. Major White was not only receptive, he was very impressed.

"Cohn," he said to me one day. "You could sell rotten tomatoes."

The words of this strange compliment have stayed with me for life. Although I never did sell rotten tomatoes, Major White's comment became my personal logo. I realized that I possessed an optimistic and resilient attitude, the positive result of being forced to manage myself under unfortunate circumstances—the loss of my mother, the hardships of life in Hongkew, and being on my own since the age of fourteen.

Major White's words—*Cohn, you could sell rotten tomatoes*—often echoed within me, reminding me that each person has something to offer. I suspected that in future opportunities the product I'd be challenged to sell would be myself.

Unfortunately for me, Major White's tour of duty was coming to an end. He could hardly wait to leave, go home to America, return to Texas as a civilian, and be with his family. When it was time to say goodbye, he put his hand on my shoulder.

"Hans," he said, "if you ever get to Texas, look me up, will you?"

I appreciated his friendly gesture.

Now that the war was over, I too dreamed of coming to America. In fact, when my family left Berlin, we had planned originally to come to the United States. We imagined then that Shanghai would be a temporary home until our quota number for immigration came up. When World War II broke out just four months after we moved to Shanghai, we never dreamed it would continue for six long years or that we would have such a long wait before immigrating.

The Shanghai ghetto was being disbanded at last, but Jewish refugees still remained stateless, displaced persons. Where should we go? That was the question on everyone's mind. Survivors didn't want to remain in China because the Red Army of Mao Tze Tung was advancing toward Shanghai. Russian Jews, who escaped the Russian Revolution, had no use for Communism, and wanted to go elsewhere. Only very few Berlin Jews found it appealing to return to Germany; most of us were embittered after learning how Hitler slaughtered our people.

Maybe America? Would the land of freedom and liberty take stateless refugees? Everyone was seeking a sense of belonging, and I too was searching for where I could, finally, create my own roots. One day in the summer of 1946 I learned that three hundred Shanghai refugees with Australian relatives had received immigration papers. In Shanghai they were scheduled to board the Matson Line's *General Gordon*, which was chartered to meet in Hong Kong the *Dantroon*, the troop ship that would then sail to Sydney and Melbourne.

Suddenly I saw my chance. Determined to take life into my own hands and get out of Shanghai, I decided to sneak on board the *General Gordon*. It was a daring attempt, but my youth and a desire for adventure gave me the courage to surreptitiously leave China. Without saying goodbye to my father, I put a brief farewell note under his pillow while he was out of the apartment. Then I disappeared, never divulging my destination. In spite of a guilty conscience I was, nevertheless, on my way.

It was only much later, after I was in America, that I learned from Shanghai friends who knew my father that he cried bitter tears after discovering my note. To this day I feel remorseful about my action. Many unresolved questions still haunt me about leaving Shanghai and my father without even saying goodbye. I sometimes wondered why I left so suddenly, but a resolute voice within me had insisted, demanding *I have to do it, I have to do it.*

On the solemn Jewish holiday of Yom Kippur, the Day of Atonement, we ask to be forgiven for sins we have committed. Back in 1946 I thought to myself there was still time to ask forgiveness. I wanted so much to talk to my father and be forgiven.

Only later I learned that by 1948 the last Jews left Shanghai. Some came to the U.S. because President Truman allowed 100,000 Jews to enter. Even so, the American quota system was still so difficult that many Jews went instead to other countries. My father went to England but did come to America under the Polish quota a few years after I did. Although I had the best intentions to bare my innermost feelings to him, alas, the right moment never came and we never did speak about my leaving.

# AUSTRALIA

## Chapter Fifteen

# Daring

With a pounding heart I joined the group of refugees boarding the *General Gordon*, the ship that would at last take me away from Shanghai and bring me to new opportunities in Australia, the land "down under."

No officials were checking people onto the ship, so I casually ascended the gangplank. Pretending to wave goodbye to someone on the dock, I succeeded in sneaking on board as a stowaway—without papers or luggage, but carrying only a bag with my prayer book and a change of underwear.

The ship's siren blasted and all visitors were ordered to leave the boat, but I remained as the *General Gordon* pulled away from the dock. Two of my friends, passengers who had papers, knew I was a stowaway. They not only gave me moral support as my adventurous voyage began, but also let me stay in their stateroom for the two-day journey from Shanghai to Kowloon, Hong Kong.

I excitedly looked forward to stowing away on the *Dantroon*. I felt confident I'd succeed again because so far everything seemed to be going so smoothly. But in Kowloon a rude surprise awaited when an agent informed the Shanghai refugees that although the *Dantroon* had been summoned from Japan, its orders were changed.

"The *Dantroon* will sail to Sydney to pick up American servicemen bound for the States," he announced. "So we regret to inform you that your trip is canceled. You will have to remain in Hong Kong and make other arrangements to get to Australia."

What now? I wondered. Fortunately, the Kadoorie family, who aided us when we first arrived in Shanghai, helped once more in Hong Kong. As owners of the famous Peninsula Hotel, they offered us food and temporary lodging. The hotel ballroom literally became a refugee camp for three hundred Shanghai Jews. In those days Hong Kong was under strict British rule, and I knew it would be dangerous to remain there illegally. The other refugees understood I was a stow-away, but they didn't divulge any information to the authorities.

After two weeks, I learned that the SS *Yuchow*, a small 3000-ton British freighter, was heading for Australia. The ship had British officers, a Chinese crew that didn't speak English, and capacity for carrying only fifty passengers—with proper visas. Nevertheless, the following day I decided to try my luck once again and sneak aboard, this time assisted by Billy Antman, a school friend from Shanghai.

When the ship headed out for the Philippine Islands, the first destination, I breathed a sigh of cautious relief. (All the other refugees who were left behind in Hong Kong, I found out later, eventually managed to make arrangements to leave.)

The weather at sea was atrocious. The water was especially rough passing the Philippines. Rainstorms and typhoons tossed the small ship about and the majority of passengers became extremely seasick. Because most of them were sitting on the deck, trying to recover, the little dining room was almost empty during mealtimes. Fortunately, I wasn't seasick and since no one else was hungry, it was easy for me to get fed. In fact, I felt so secure I even volunteered to lead Sabbath Eve services for the passengers on deck. Out of curiosity, the British captain attended and was very impressed with my fine singing voice and my knowledge of the Hebrew liturgy. He even shook my hand and complimented me.

In the meantime, as we approached the coast of New Guinea the inclement weather improved. The sea was blue and calm and as we sailed smoothly under a beautiful sky, the passengers' appetites returned. In the dining room, though, the head count revealed fifty-one passengers on board instead of fifty. When the Chinese waiter promptly reported the discrepancy to the purser, sudden panic set in and my fellow refugees feared we might all be sent back to Hong Kong. Consequently, to allay their fears, I gave myself up.

This time the previously cordial captain was furious when he saw me.

"You had some nerve," he said angrily. "If it wouldn't be for your good voice and the nice Hebrew songs," he yelled, "I should throw you to the sharks!"

He immediately sent a cable to the immigration authorities in Sydney, reporting "Stowaway on board!"

The Sydney officials inquired, "What papers does he have?"

"No papers," was the reply.

"Then keep him in custody," the officials ordered.

Two days later, the SS *Yuchow* arrived in Sydney. While the passengers disembarked, overjoyed to find a safe haven in a new, free country, I was locked inside a staff cabin. My fate was yet to be decided, but I feared that my next destination might be a return trip to Hong Kong.

*Chapter Sixteen*

# The Escape

The thought of returning to China made me shudder.

What awaited me in Hong Kong, I knew, was nothing less than an extended jail sentence and perhaps even worse. Many people, I had heard, didn't survive the communicable diseases in prison as well as the typically harsh conditions.

Lying in my cabin, depressed about my future, I was suddenly startled when a ship's officer unlocked my door and permitted a well-dressed gentleman to enter. I was fearful initially but when the visitor shook my hand, his friendly gesture persuaded me to relax.

"My name is Brand," he said, introducing himself, "and I represent the Jewish Welfare Society of Sydney. I've come to help you."

He seemed compassionate, which evoked a spark of optimism that I might be released from my confinement.

"Listen, young man," he said, leaning toward me. "Tonight I shall fly to Canberra to obtain a residence permit for you."

My eyes lit up. I was incredulous. If he were actually going to travel to the capital of Australia and see an immigration official, then maybe there really was hope for me.

"Tomorrow this ship sails for Melbourne. Behave yourself and don't do anything foolish," Brand cautioned.

I could hardly contain myself. Until then, I had pictured myself languishing, despondent in a Chinese jail.

"In Melbourne you'll be met by one of our secretaries, while I try to procure the necessary papers. Until then God bless you."

With those words, he turned and left. The ship's officer locked me in again, and that was the last I saw of Mr. Brand.

The *Yuchow* left Sydney, passing under the famous Harbor Bridge. Peering through the porthole, I admired the beautiful waterfront of Australia—so close and yet so far. The sky was blue, the sea calm, and it was September, just before 5707, the Jewish New Year of 1946. From my pocket I took out my little prayer book and started to pray. What else could I do?

The next day, as the ship entered the Melbourne harbor, my heart raced in eager anticipation, expecting to be freed. When the ship's anchor dropped, the engines came to a halt and longshoremen came aboard to unload and load cargo. Again a ship's officer surprised me by unlocking my cabin, and a young man from the Welfare Society stepped in. The grim expression on his face told me something was wrong. Sure enough, he began telling me, "I'm afraid," he said, "we have bad news for you, Hans."

In a voice filled with pity, he explained that Mr. Brand tried to get a visa for me but was unsuccessful. Due to upcoming elections in Australia, the Minister of Immigration didn't want to risk losing the election by sticking his neck out on my account.

"You'll have to return to Hong Kong," he continued. "But we'll do what we can to have you admitted to Australia later—legally." Then he reached into his pocket and handed me a ten-pound note. I was too stunned even to express thanks.

"Have a happy New Year," he said. I was still speechless in misery.

Before I knew it, he seemed to have vanished. Once again the door closed, I heard the key turned in the lock, and I was alone and desolate in my cabin. What had been a glimmer of hope turned into despair. I felt dejected, forsaken. My prayers had been in vain. Disheartened, my tears flowed copiously.

Yet, in spite of everything, I realized I was *not* ready to give up. Wiping away tears, I began to think. The ship was to sail back to China the next day. How, I wondered, could I possibly escape and avoid being arrested in Hong Kong?

At five P.M. a steward brought my evening meal. My stomach was in such knots I had no appetite, but the silverware on the tray suddenly gave me an idea. Picking up the knife, I set about working on the lock of the cabin door, feverishly attempting to loosen the screws. Success! It worked! Surveying the cabin, I spotted a small electric fan affixed to the wall. Scraping some oil from the motor, I smeared it over my face.

I was nervous but determined to make a break.

The sun was beginning to set when I cautiously sneaked out, taking only my little prayer book and the ten-pound note, both tucked into my pocket. Edging toward the front of the ship, which was tied up against the dock, I jumped over, landing ten feet down to solid ground. Again, I was lucky—no broken bones or sprains.

Looking quite messy, with bedraggled clothing and a dirty, greasy face, I was not recognized and mingled among the dock workers, then on their way home. Agitated and feeling my heart beating very fast, I hurried to get far away from the ship.

It was getting dark and I was finally on my way. I was free! And that was how the Jewish year 5706 was coming to an end for me.

## Chapter Seventeen

# The First Day Down Under

Walking briskly away from the waterfront, I headed toward where I saw streetcars, or trams, as Australians called them. With palpitating heart and agitated stomach, I jumped on a tram, not caring where it was going. Anywhere would do as long as it was away from the *S.S. Yuchow.*

The tram had gone only a short distance when the conductor came through to collect the fare, which was three pence. Having no change, of course, I pulled out my ten-pound note. By today's standards that would be like presenting a one-hundred dollar bill to pay for a ten-cent fare.

The conductor eyed me suspiciously, then mumbled, "I have no change," and he waved me off. Nervous and fearful of attracting attention, I got off the tram and began walking aimlessly. I had no idea where I was but knew I was looking for the Carlton district because a Shanghai friend had given me the address of a Jewish family who lived in that area.

Suddenly I saw a neon sign that said "Carlton" and happily told myself I must be on the right track. But to my disappointment, coming closer to the sign I realized it was just an advertisement for Australia's most popular beer, which happened to be called "Carlton Ale."

I was tired, hungry, and aware that the sky was rapidly getting dark. But it was the eve of Rosh Hashana, and knowing that a New Year was beginning, I felt strengthened in my determination to keep going, to find my way and not give up. A few blocks later another sign at an intersection caught my eye: Cohen's Kosher Restaurant. Gathering up my courage, I walked in to ask for help, anticipating that since my name was also Cohn, I might find some compassion there.

Mr. Cohen, the owner, stood by the door, greeting each of the beautifully attired guests with "*Good Yontif*, Happy New Year!"

Apprehensive but hopeful, I approached him, apologizing for my appearance, and told him about my unscheduled arrival in Australia.

He listened sympathetically, then said, "Follow me."

He led the way to the kitchen, where the smell of food reminded me that I hadn't eaten for many hours. After being introduced to Mrs. Cohen, who wore an immaculate white apron, I explained my scruffy appearance and repeated my story, which brought tears to her eyes.

"You sit down right here," she said. "Now tell me, when did you last have something to eat?"

I was an unexpected and improperly attired guest, so she pointed me to a chair in a corner of the kitchen. My gastric juices began to flow as she set before me a plate of challah and a bowl of steaming chicken soup, which both tasted marvelous.

On the kitchen radio I heard the evening news, which reported my escape from the boat, so the police already were looking for me. I pondered what my next step should be.

"We have to get you out of town," Mrs. Cohen insisted and directly went to the telephone. "I'm calling my friend Mr. Schreiber," she explained. "I'll ask if he could put you up for the night."

"Tell him I'm a good cook," I called out. "And I'm willing to work hard!"

"You can talk about that in the morning," she replied. "First, get some sleep."

Before long, Mr. Schreiber, who was not Jewish, arrived and took me to his house for the night. A kindhearted man, he listened sympathetically as I told my story once again. He was acquainted with the plight of stateless refugees, but I was the first one he had ever met.

"Hans," he began the next morning. "I know some people who own a resort hotel in Daylesford, not far from here. I wonder if they could use you in their kitchen."

He saw right away that I was extremely interested.

"I'll give them a call," he suggested. "There's no harm in asking."

Mr. Schreiber phoned the Rollers, owners of the resort, and as luck would have it, the previous evening their chef got drunk and quit his job. When the Rollers learned about me, they were thrilled.

"Bring him here! We have a place for him! Immediately!" they urged.

That very morning I was driven to Daylesford, fifteen miles from Melbourne. The Rollers greeted me as if I were a gift from heaven. Within twenty-four hours after arriving in Australia, I found myself not only with a roof over my head, but also with gainful employment as a cook.

Perhaps my prayers helped, but at any rate my faith was restored. Miracles do happen. The New Year 5707 was getting off to a good start.

## Chapter Eighteen

# A Special Connection

The next morning I began my new life in Daylesford by picking up the Melbourne newspaper. The headline startled me.

### STOWAWAY ESCAPES FROM SHIP AT DOCK

Since the police were already looking for me as Hans Cohn, I knew the only way to avoid being arrested was to assume a different name. After giving the matter considerable thought I decided from then on to be known as *Johnny Korn*. I chose *Johnny* because *Hans* is also *Johan*, which is German for *John*. I chose *Korn* because it was so similar to *Cohn*.

As the Rollers' chef I worked very hard and I adjusted quickly to my new surroundings. Having lived in Shanghai amid squalid surroundings for seven years, I literally felt that arriving in Australia was like coming to a land of milk and honey. During the war everything was scarce and expensive but here food was abundant. I gorged myself with milk shakes and ice cream, gaining weight practically overnight.

The fresh air of the Australian countryside was invigorating and the scenery magnificent—golden wheat fields, flowers in bloom, wide-open spaces, and free-roaming sheep (more sheep than people). I felt like I was in paradise. Little could the police imagine where I was—standing behind the stove in an Aussie country hotel in the small village of Daylesford.

The ten-pound note I had been given aboard the *Yuchow* came in handy because I urgently needed to buy new clothes. With my first salary in hand, I proudly entered the local bank to open an account. Since I used my new name, there was no problem.

The Rollers' hotel was small, so I mingled freely with the guests. They didn't have even the slightest inkling that the young man casually sitting in the garden during breaks was wanted by the police. Luckily there were no photographs, so I felt safe and unafraid.

Life was good. One of the hotel guests was an accomplished pianist who happened to have a book of Schubert *Lieder* with him, and one evening after dinner we met to do some singing. After a few weeks in Daylesford, I no longer felt like a stranger. But it soon was evident to others that I was not run-of-the-mill kitchen help. That's when people became suspicious.

"Where were you born, Johnny?" one curious guest quizzed me. "And what made you come to this little village?"

His questions were perfectly reasonable. After all, except for Elizabeth, the boss's daughter, there was no one around my age to socialize with. She was a charming girl with an attractive face. Because she had a limp, I suspected she must have had polio as a child.

Another guest asked, "Isn't it unusual for a young man like you to come to such a small town? What is there for you to do here?"

In response, I made up all sorts of excuses—like enjoying the peaceful countryside, or wanting to get away from big cities, and so on. But such questions started to worry me. I did not want to be detected. The war was over, yet I felt that complete freedom still wasn't mine to enjoy. I wondered if maybe my life in Australia was just an illusion—being down under, far away from Nazi Germany, but also wanted by the authorities, when my only crime was wanting to be free.

It was time, I decided, to move on.

The Rollers were disappointed when I told them of my plan. They hated to see me leave, and so did Elizabeth. She and I had become friends in a short time. Nevertheless, I had to look for greener and safer pastures, so my new destination was Sydney. Years later I was saddened to learn that Elizabeth had committed suicide.

Since I had saved up a few Australian pounds from my job, I could afford to fly from Melbourne to Sydney. A friend drove me to the airport, snapped my photo, and I boarded a Qantas propeller plane for my first airplane trip. The magnificent Sydney harbor was even more spectacular from the air.

Once in Sydney I rented a small apartment and opened a bank account with my savings from Daylesford. Then I marched over to David Jones, the city's leading department store on Pitts Street, and purchased a beautiful shirt, tie, and pin-striped suit.

Soon an old adage proved true: "It's not what you know, it's who you know." A special connection, I often found, comes in very handy. Through an acquaintance, I was introduced to Dr. Porush, Sydney's distinguished Chief

Rabbi of the Modern Orthodox Great Synagogue, the biggest in Australia. He helped me to make contacts and also invited me to his home for Friday night dinner, following the Jewish tradition of inviting guests for the Sabbath.

To make a good impression, I arrived in my brand new suit with a fresh haircut and scrubbed face. I was overjoyed to be in the presence of a famous rabbi and be received royally by his family. Again I told my story, and when the rabbi learned that I could sing and knew the synagogue liturgy, he contacted Werner Baer, his choir director, also from Berlin. I could hardly believe it, that on the very next Sabbath I not only met the director, but also sat in the synagogue loft as a new member of the mixed choir.

Rabbi Porush also introduced me to the owner of the biggest catering firm in Sydney at that time, Walter Magnus. He hired me as a cook for his Elite Catering business and I began work immediately. The following week I found myself in the kitchen of the Government House, catering a dinner in honor of Winston Churchill, who was visiting Australia. I stood by the broiler, cooking two hundred *Filet Mignon Rossini*, tenderloin steaks wrapped in bacon and topped with liver pate. Although I did not get to see Mr. Churchill, the whole experience seemed like a dream.

As Johnny Korn, I hoped to make a fresh beginning again, this time in Sydney. Although uneasy about the continuing newspaper accounts describing the police searches for Hans Cohn, in general I felt that so far, luck had certainly been on my side.

## Chapter Nineteen

# Between Darkness and Light

It didn't take me long to adapt to a new environment in Sydney. As Johnny Korn I ventured forth to dances at the Jewish Center and soon made friends. In the synagogue choir I was welcome and accepted as a sonorous bass. As a single young man, I soon found myself invited to homes for Sabbath and holiday meals, especially where there were eligible daughters in the family. Those were pleasant days.

Although my new alias went over easily with other people, it was getting hard for me to accept myself. My real name was a secret known only to the Australian authorities. Notices about "Hans Cohn" appeared regularly in the newspapers as the police continued to hunt me down. In fact, a warrant had been issued for my arrest.

Frequently I had to tell little white lies to avoid divulging my true identity. Only Rabbi Porush and Mr. Brand, from the Jewish Welfare Society, knew the whole story—that I was both Hans Cohn *and* Johnny Korn. My days consisted of happy moments only to end with restless nights. I didn't sleep well. I knew something had to be done to change the situation. After all, how long can one go on leading a double life?

I even began to wonder why I had come to these shores in the first place, especially since I had left my father behind when I escaped from Shanghai. By getting myself to Australia and taking control of my own destiny, I had hoped to have my father join me. With my present illegal status, that was no longer possible. In addition, though, my father's immigration status then was still very complicated. He came under the Polish immigration quota because after Germany lost World War I, Poland annexed Posen, his German birthplace. My father's quota number for the U.S. was in the thousands, so instead of waiting several years for an American visa he went to England instead.

After six months in Australia as Johnny Korn, I decided to see Mr. Brand at the Jewish Welfare Society to explore how to resolve my predicament. He listened attentively and sympathetically to my dilemma, but his answer left little doubt.

"There's only one way out, Hans. Give yourself up to the authorities," he advised. "I'll do my best to intervene on your behalf and get you a permit so you can remain here in Australia."

When I consulted Rabbi Porush, he concurred with Mr. Brand. The following morning Mr. Brand escorted me to the immigration authorities. Wanting to appear serious and mature, I wore my new suit and tie. The officer on duty received us courteously, but had little sympathy for my case.

"Since you're an illegal immigrant," the official declared, "you'll have to be tried in our court."

Perhaps I was less intimidated than I might otherwise have been because I had learned of a curious loophole. According to an archaic Australian law, an illegal immigrant who can successfully pass a test in a given foreign language would be granted a residence permit. I spoke a few languages—German, French, Chinese, Yiddish, and English—so I had high hopes the authorities would choose one I knew and eagerly awaited their decision. I was astonished when they chose Portuguese! By selecting a language totally unfamiliar to me, I understood they were intentionally preventing me from staying in the country.

My situation appeared hopeless and became even worse when I was sentenced to six months in the city jail for entering Australia illegally! I went totally numb and struggled to hold back tears. Mr. Brand sat taciturn and motionless. He too was flabbergasted.

"Don't give up, Hans," he consoled, putting his hand on my shoulder. "I'll fly to Canberra immediately and talk again to Mr. Caldwell, the Minister of Immigration. He might intervene on your behalf."

It was almost noon when Mr. Brand left hurriedly to catch the next plane to Australia's capital. Meanwhile, I remained locked up in the courthouse prison. I sat quietly, but felt uncomfortable surrounded by a group of arrested criminals, in prison garb, awaiting trial for various offenses. They looked skeptically at me, immaculately dressed in my best clothes, curious to know who I was and what I was doing there.

The big story of the day was a major jewelry heist in Sydney.

"What're you in fer, mate?" one of the felons asked me with a big grin, "Was it you who pulled off that big one?"

Once again I told my story, which must have sounded very peculiar to these fellows, who were quite disinterested. To them, a holdup or a burglary was more exciting and lucrative than a mundane case of illegal immigration.

While they discussed their own escapades, I felt wretched, wondering about my dreary future.

At five P.M., two guards arrived to transfer me to the Sydney City Jail. I must have looked quite strange—an elegantly dressed passenger in a black paddy wagon. Never having been in jail before and as a novice in the world of crime, I had no idea what to expect next and wondered what prison food and accommodations would be like.

The first stop was on the ground floor at the Office of Admittance, where I was duly registered, fingerprinted, handed a bag for my clothes and valuables, and given a striped uniform in exchange for my pinstriped suit. Fortunately, no mirror was available for me to behold my drastically different attire.

I was about to be led to the elevator and assigned to my new home—a cell—when a breathless Mr. Brand appeared, briefcase in hand. At the last moment he had somehow produced a two-hundred pound bond that the Jewish Welfare Society posted for my release. The bond included a six-month permit allowing me to remain in Australia. Within that period I was to leave the country, but could, if I wished, apply later for permission to enter Australia again as a legal immigrant.

Between tears and laughter I changed clothes once again, no longer caring that my suit, shirt and tie were now wrinkled. I was relieved and exhausted. By then it was starting to get dark and Mr. Brand kindly drove me home. On that eventful night, I went to bed as Hans Cohn again, but this time as a legal, temporary resident.

What was the next step? The answer would have to wait until morning. Another chapter of my life was unfolding. Overcome by happy dreams, I welcomed much needed sleep. After a period of darkness, I was beginning to see some light.

# Chapter Twenty

# Waltzing Matilda

The next morning, I awoke refreshed after sleeping longer than usual—my first restful night in a long time. Months of anxiety about my status were finally behind me. My trial was over, my jail sentence suspended, and I had six more months before leaving Sydney. The sun shone brightly through the bedroom window, and I felt relieved and calm as I set off for my job as a cook.

At that time I was working at a fine French restaurant called *Le Coq D'Or* after "The Golden Rooster," an opera by Rimski Korsakov. Through people at the Great Synagogue, I had met the French couple who owned it. The wife, who was the chef, took a liking to me and I learned much from her including how to cook with wine, mushrooms, and sour cream. To this day, I can produce the finest Beef Stroganoff based on her Parisian recipe.

When I first came to Australia, I intended to stay, but after realizing I'd have to leave the country within six months, I contacted Martin Cohn, my father's cousin in Los Angeles. In a letter I explained my situation, asking him to send me an immigration affidavit, a sworn statement guaranteeing that I would not become a burden to the U.S. Uncle Martin graciously complied with my request, so I was able to get a visa to America from the U.S. consul in Sydney.

The process was easy for me because although I was still considered stateless, the Australian Ministry of Immigration had issued me a Certificate of Identity with a photo, verifying that I was born in Berlin and therefore a German national. After the war Germany's quota was wide open and undersubscribed because, as America's former enemies, German nationals were restricted for immigration unless they could prove they had not been Nazis. So I had no problem that way.

But when I went to the Matson Line office to purchase a ticket for departure within the next six months, the clerk gave me dismal news. He informed me, regretfully, that war brides who were marrying Yanks got preference for tickets, so ships were booked up for the following ten months. Ten months! By then, my residence permit would have expired and I'd be deported. Or I'd have to go back to jail. Once again my wings were clipped when I received that bad news.

Frantic, I called Mr. Brand—my guardian angel—and he accompanied me to the shipping office, where he knew the general manager. We marched past the clerk I had spoken with earlier and straight into the manager's office. Mr. Brand did the talking this time and clearly he was very persuasive because after just a few minutes, the general manager turned to me.

"When do you want to leave, young man?" "Within the next three months, I hope," I replied with trepidation.

"Could you be ready next week?" he asked in all seriousness.

For a moment I was too astounded to speak. Then, ecstatic, I answered, "Certainly, Sir!"

To my great surprise I left the office with a ticket in my hand. That very same week was to be my last in Australia. Especially on such short notice, I felt a wave of sadness about having to depart so suddenly from the country I enjoyed living in for one year. I was having a wonderful experience. I loved Australia's leisurely pace and thrived on life in the enchanting city of Sydney, where my weekends had such a special quality.

On Saturdays I sang my heart out in the Great Synagogue choir, but above all I listened wholeheartedly to the cantor. Vicariously I saw myself standing at a pulpit, dressed in a clerical robe, leading a congregation in prayer. Although I hadn't even finished high school at that time, I dreamed that some day I would have the opportunity to study and actually fulfill my aspiration.

At that time, Australia had Blue Laws, which meant everything was closed on Sundays except for churches and private clubs. For my friends and me, however, Sunday was an especially active day. We often met at Bondi Beach, one of the many world-class beaches with which Sydney is blessed. I also visited with friends at the Jewish Club, which was similar to today's Jewish Community Centers. We enjoyed music, games, lectures, and refreshments.

I knew I would soon miss the famous Sydney Harbor Bridge, a unique landmark, and the Botanical Gardens, bathed in sunshine and located by the waterfront. I often walked in the park there amid flora and fauna, enjoying the breathtaking view of the harbor filled with ships and sailboats. I cherished the many times I took a lunch bag and listened to free symphony concerts at the city hall—before the world famous Sydney Opera House existed.

As the time came for me to say goodbye to Australia, I bid a fond farewell to the wonderful people I met through the synagogue and the Jewish Club. Most of all I was sad to leave these friends, who expected me to later return to Sydney and become a legitimate Aussie. Why not, I had thought to myself earlier. Australia was a beautiful country with a bright future. We sang, danced, and finished up with the old Australian Bush song—"The Jolly Swagman."

I was quite familiar with the song, but it wasn't until I left Australia that I properly understood its lyrics. The *Jolly Swagman* refers to an Australian itinerant, a hobo, or possibly a bum. The *swag* is a bundle that contains all his possessions. The *Billabong* is a dried-up riverbed. "*Matilda*" in the chorus is another word for *swag*.

Like many folk songs that contain a deeper meaning, this one conveys strong feelings and is supposedly sung by a tough man. I could well identify with it.

> "... *Waltzing Matilda, Waltzing Matilda*
> *You'll come a-waltzing Matilda with me.*
> *And his ghost may be heard*
> *As you ride beside the billabong,*
> *You'll come a-waltzing, Matilda, with me...*"

All my belongings still fitted into one suitcase so it took me no time to pack. In September 1947—one year after arriving in Australia—I boarded the American Liberty Ship *SS Marine Phoenix*, a C-4 troop carrier, as a legitimate passenger bound for San Francisco.

# CALIFORNIA

## Chapter Twenty-One

# San Francisco, Here I Come

The twenty-three day sea journey concluded as the *S.S. Marine Phoenix* arrived in the United States at six in the morning on October 14, 1947. After a sleepless night, I stood on deck eagerly watching our entrance into San Francisco Bay. In the distance a foghorn sounded and as our ship approached, a local pilot came on board to guide us into the harbor and to our designated pier for disembarking.

This time, facing an immigration officer didn't worry me because I came proudly as a legal immigrant. With an entrance permit, one suitcase of clothing, no valuables, and eighty dollars in cash, I confidently walked down the gangplank. Many passengers, especially the Australian war brides, arrived and received a rousing reception from family and friends. But no one was there in San Francisco to welcome me.

My destination was Los Angeles, where Uncle Martin awaited me. Since I intended to take the night train from San Francisco, I had only one day in the city to sightsee, but that short visit was like a dream. All of a sudden I was in America! San Francisco seemed so elegant and the people more formal than in Australia, but there was a nostalgic resemblance between Sydney's Harbor and the San Francisco Bay. By the time I hopped on a Gray Line Tour, the morning fog had lifted and I beheld the famous Golden Gate Bridge in all its glory. We passed the impressive Temple Emanu-El, a beautiful edifice. Little did I imagine that twenty years later I would be invited to sing there. In San Francisco's Chinatown, the smells and sights brought back many memories of my life in Shanghai.

In the evening, after a tiring, but exhilarating day of touring, I came to the train station. Since my finances were limited, I purchased the cheapest ticket on the Starlight Train, leaving San Francisco at midnight and arriving at Los

Angeles in the morning. I was so excited about being in America and about meeting my Cohn relatives again that for the second night in a row, I couldn't sleep.

In Los Angeles, I bought a bouquet of roses for Uncle Martin and Aunt Martha, who were also fairly new German immigrants, but they had come to the U.S. from Brazil. Grabbing a cab to their modest home in Hollywood, I arrived and rang the doorbell, feeling dead tired and droopy. Uncle Martin, a man in his early seventies, welcomed me warmly. I handed over the roses, a small token of gratitude and thanks both for their affidavit, which helped me come to America, as well as for the food and lodging they offered me.

"Put down your suitcase, Hans," he greeted me, "And take a shower while we fix you some breakfast."

Then came the lecture, which I hadn't expected. Uncle Martin began to paint a gloomy picture about the current economy.

"Listen, Hans, don't be bamboozled by what you heard about this country in Australia," he warned in his imperfect English. "Now the war is over. Life here is tough. Jobs are hard to find. Thousands of soldiers are coming home. They're all trying to find work."

He didn't give me a chance to get a word in.

"Let's take a ride and find out what the situation is," Martin insisted, apparently not noticing that I was exhausted.

The last thing I wanted to do was to go out, but I had no choice. We took the streetcar on Santa Monica Boulevard, rode downtown, and got off in the business district to begin our search. An imposing figure, Uncle Martin was a tall man and not the least bit shy. We stopped at the first restaurant to try our luck.

"Follow me, Hans," he instructed, opening the door to the establishment. I stood behind him as he shouted with a heavy Berlinese accent, "Hallow . . . I have good cook here. Have you job for him?"

I could see the clientele seated at the tables thought he was some kind of lunatic. It was the most embarrassing experience I ever endured. I felt like running back to Australia. A few more restaurants—the same story all over again—and, not surprisingly, no takers.

"You see, my boy? You see how difficult it is?" Martin said in German, trying to prove his case. By then I could hardly keep my eyes open. I begged to go home so I could get some sleep.

The next morning I took matters into my own hands. Contrary to Martin's approach, I understood that the logical approach was to get a newspaper and look in the help-wanted ads. I left the Cohn house and returned an hour later.

"You back already?" Uncle Martin was surprised and curious.

"Yes, I came to get my cook's uniform out of my suitcase. I'm starting work."

Martin was right that jobs were hard to find, but in the food line I always found employment. My first position in America was as a short order cook at a New York-style delicatessen on Hollywood and Vine Streets. The place was open around the clock and I was hired for the graveyard shift at ten dollars a day. Because I was inexperienced and wanted to learn the ropes, I volunteered to also work the previous eight-hour shift.

Suddenly I found a brand new language thrown at me, and speed was imperative to keep up.

"Two CB (corned beef) sans on rye, hold the mayo, fry two over easy. Hold the bacon."

Hold the bacon? I didn't know where to hold the bacon. Order slips? They were scribbled, resembling a doctor's prescription. I did my best while trying to keep watching to see what the cook on duty was doing. When midnight came my regular shift began and then I was completely on my own.

"One liverwurst san to go," A waitress yelled out. When I put it on a plate, she retorted, "I said *to go.*"

"Well, *let's go!*" I yelled back at her.

The kind dishwasher was my interpreter. "Hey, man, *to go* means wrap it up to take out."

The waitress was furious with me and I felt my face turn red, but I improved quickly. After three days I rented a furnished room for ten dollars a week. I knew Martin was worried that I might be dependent on them since he had signed the affidavit for me. Unfortunately, I lasted only eight days on that first job. The owner fired me because he found someone better. He probably was right.

Across the street, the Pantages Theater Restaurant had a sign in the window: Busboy Wanted. I applied, was hired on the spot, and began work immediately. The pay was less than at the Deli but all my meals were included. It was great and I was happy to have a job. While clearing tables I frequently hummed a tune and as luck would have it, one day a guest noticed and engaged me in conversation.

"You have a nice voice. Did you ever study singing?"

It was Dr. Robert Davis, the former husband of Amy McPherson, the famous Evangelist. Davis was a well-known organist and voice teacher, and the very next day I was in his studio as a new student. My busboy salary was six dollars a day and each weekly lesson was five dollars, but I managed. Dr. Davis and I hit it off well. He knew many movie stars and being eager to help, referred me to a restaurant in Burbank, "The Ryan Pan," owned by Peggy Ryan, a dancer. Together with Donald O'Connor and Jack Oakie, she had recently completed a movie called "The Merry Monahans."

Just at that time Peggy was looking for a chef in her restaurant, which featured New Orleans cuisine, primarily seafood—oysters, lobster, and shrimp. I applied for the job. She had her doubts about engaging me because I was only twenty-one.

I must have thought then of Major White's words: *Cohn, you could sell rotten tomatoes.*

Getting up my courage I said, "I'm a good cook, Miss Ryan. And I'll be glad to work a few days for free if you'll just give me a chance."

Peggy agreed and after two days in her kitchen, she hired me at ninety dollars a week. Although I had never attended a culinary institute or school for chefs, I had always been around food and learned with my eyes. I was able to study a cookbook, research recipes at the library, and from then on I was self-made. I picked up a little bit here and a little bit there, then added my own ingenuity and imagination.

Working for Peggy was the chance of a lifetime. On my day off I continued studying voice and also took piano lessons.

Life in America was great!

## Chapter Twenty-Two

# Greetings from Uncle Sam

It didn't take me long to make a niche for myself in Los Angeles.

In Peggy's restaurant my culinary skills made a big hit and her guests ate enthusiastically. I always preferred French, European, or Jewish cuisine, and Peggy was pleased when I introduced a few of my special dishes such as Hungarian Goulash, *Coq au Vin,* and especially Beef Stroganoff, prepared the way I learned in Sydney.

After several weeks on the job, Peggy invited me to move into her little guesthouse at the rear of the restaurant, so overnight I practically became a member of the Ryan family. Being so easily available, I felt a bit obligated to her, but on the other hand ninety dollars a week was a lot in 1947, especially including room and board.

Although I was the chef, Peggy also employed a black cook who taught me how to make New Orleans-style dishes like Chicken Gumbo and Lobster Thermidor. Eager to expand my repertory, I went to a local bookstore and purchased a book about New Orleans Creole cooking. After mastering the primitive stoves in Shanghai and the improved ones in Australia, I especially enjoyed Peggy's kitchen. It was the most up-to-date kitchen I had ever worked in, and I enjoyed getting acquainted with equipment such as electric mixers for mashing and machines for washing dishes.

In addition to cooking, I also learned to order food, a critical skill in the restaurant business. Although I knew about quantities, I didn't know where to make contacts or find sources for vegetables and other foods. Peggy's father, Jimmy Ryan, was very helpful to me in the beginning. Somehow I had the kind of personality or perhaps a sense of humility that made people realize I was not a "wise guy." It was easy for me to be nice to people, and they were always helpful to me. All my life, in fact, I've been fortunate to meet nice people.

The Ryan Pan, located on Olive Avenue in the San Fernando Valley, catered to many movie stars, primarily Peggy's friends who sometimes stopped by the kitchen to compliment me on my cooking and food presentation. One evening Peggy came in with several other people, just to say hello.

"Hans, I want you to meet my friends, Betty, Donald, and Jackie."

"Hi," I said nonchalantly, not realizing who they were. To my surprise, the friends were Betty Grable, Donald O'Connor, and Jackie Coogan. I was in awe when Betty Grable, looking extremely glamorous, complimented me on my Lobster Thermidor.

"You're such a great cook," she murmured, "I'd love to take you home with me!"

With my first savings from working at the Ryan Pan, I bought a 1937 Plymouth convertible for $400 with $100 down. The first evening I was so excited to drive I was tempted to spend the entire night in the car. Los Angeles thrilled me with how much it had to offer. The Shrine Auditorium had a great Opera season, and nearby the Hollywood Bowl featured the L.A. Philharmonic, conducted by Alfred Wallenstein. Often, after work around nine o'clock in the evening, I would drive down to the Palladium Ballroom in Hollywood where for two dollars one could dance to the big bands. With no shortage of girls, it was always easy to find a partner. Work, music lessons, entertainment, and late night reading filled my life.

For spiritual nourishment I went to a Conservative synagogue in Burbank whenever I had time. Since the congregation had no cantor, the members especially appreciated my volunteering to lead some services. Jewish music and prayer still touched me, and my lifelong dream was to become a cantor. Thankfully in Los Angeles my musical repertoire grew with a variety of songs. After seeing "The Jazz Singer" with Al Jolson, a cantor's son, I was so inspired I couldn't sleep that night. I knew I must sing or die. I imitated Al Jolson and memorized all his famous pieces. "You Made Me Love You" and "April Showers" were my favorites.

I learned many Jewish songs, operatic arias in various languages, and a number of German *Lieder*. Being in Hollywood, I had ambition and hoped to be discovered as a singing star. Every time I performed "Old Man River," the hit song of my life, it was a show-stopper because—with a vocal range of two and a half octaves—I could sing both baritone and bass. In spite of my musical ambitions, though, it didn't take me long to realize that Hollywood was already overflowing with talent. No one was out there waiting for me.

Even with all my activities, there was a void in my life. Being by myself at night was lonely. I had no family of my own other than Uncle Martin, and I yearned to settle down. Although I had many dates, real happiness eluded me, and I still dreamed of getting the education the Nazis had deprived me of.

Also, my memories of the war years lingered on as the political situation in the world drastically changed. I was elated when in 1948 the State of Israel was established, finally a haven for those Jews who survived the Nazi era.

America's Marshall Plan helped bring the European nations to their feet and also strengthened the Allies. To secure peace in Europe, NATO was created. Nevertheless, the Soviets were determined to disseminate their doctrine of Communism. Germany was still divided into four sectors. Berlin, according to the Potsdam Conference, was located in the Russian zone, but administered by the Allies.

In March of 1948 the Russian army, under Stalin's orders, isolated Berlin, blocking all the routes to it. Intending to force the Allies to withdraw by totally occupying the city, Stalin fomented an international crisis. By literally trying to starve the Berlin population, he almost threatened World War III. President Truman was furious.

"We are going to stay in Berlin—period," he said adamantly.

In 1949 the Berlin blockade resulted in an unprecedented airlift as American planes—around the clock—dropped 13,000 tons of food daily to save Berlin and its inhabitants. Backed by Congress, President Truman ordered a military draft.

Since I was of military age (as was every male up to age twenty-three), I was required to register with the Burbank Draft Board. As an immigrant to this country, I had to sign a paper stating that I was willing to bear arms for the U.S. At that time there was a draft lottery, and my number came up. It was the only time in my life I won a lottery, so I became one of three people in the Burbank area to receive notices to enter the army. I took and passed a test to become an officer, however, was not eligible because I wasn't yet a citizen.

The following week I received Greetings from Uncle Sam.

With mixed feelings I said goodbye to Peggy. As a farewell present, she gave me a golden Star of David on a chain, which I wear to this day. The members of the Burbank synagogue presented me with a wristwatch to express their thanks for the times I conducted services. I continued studying voice with Dr. Davis until I was drafted.

I had been in Los Angeles for only one year and perhaps because I was still an unattached young man, I recognized that although I would not have initiated any change myself, the time had come once again to move on.

# Chapter Twenty-Three

# Eva

In October of 1948 I was inducted into the American army. A military train left Los Angeles, taking me along with four hundred other draftees to Fort Ord, California. Once again I carried a single suitcase as I had done before in Germany, Shanghai, and Sydney. We traveled through the night, and although we had been given beds on the train, I barely slept, arriving at the army installation both apprehensive and excited about the new experience awaiting me.

Fort Ord was a military post with army barracks, obstacle courses, and rifle ranges. It was located on the golden coast of California, overlooking Monterey Bay. Picturesque sand dunes surrounded the Fort on one side while the other side the slopes were filled with pine trees, wild orange poppies, and natural meadows. Set between Monterey and Carmel on the west and Salinas (the lettuce bowl of America) on the east, the area was considered a vacation paradise. For me, however, it was not.

On the first day we were issued khaki uniforms, a duffel bag, and a rifle. I thought I didn't look too bad in my new outfit with my wavy, curly hair. The next day, when we were ordered to have a haircut, I remember the barber asking, "Do you want to keep that big curl in front, soldier?"

"Yes!" I said firmly.

The barber, whose own hair was not short, immediately clipped it off.

"Keep it, my boy," he said rather condescendingly, and handed the curl to me.

I was momentary stunned, shocked to see that cherished bit of hair sitting in my hand. When the barber got through with me, I looked like a jailbird. There was no charge for the haircut or the transformation.

Assigned to the 22nd Infantry Battalion, I was restricted to the post during the first three weeks of Basic Training. Life was drab. I felt lonesome, isolated, and had very little to do. The local movie house offered only B-rated movies, and three-percent beer was available in the Soldiers' Club. The nearby brothels in Watsonville didn't entice me; I never even set foot in one. Fort Ord did, however, have a marvelous library that helped me fill my evening hours, immersed in reading. Often, after a day of marching, drilling, and training to manipulate weapons, I fell asleep over a book.

About twenty Jewish soldiers were in my group and since no chaplain was on the post, we were bussed to the Salinas Temple, which advertised Jewish religious services. I volunteered as a cantor to assist the tone-deaf local rabbi, who couldn't sing a note. In order to get transportation to the synagogue, I took a test to drive an army bus, quickly obtained a license, and was able to take soldiers to the temple on Friday nights.

At that time my fellow soldiers were American-born, so they had little awareness of the Holocaust. Most people had heard mention of Auschwitz and Dachau and a few knew there were Jews in Shanghai, but the Shanghai ghetto was totally unknown. Little by little as information about the Nazis came out, people in the synagogue asked me to tell my story. My accent in English was rather difficult to identify since it was German with Chinese and British influences. I joked that I never had an accent until I came to America.

During the time I had been in glittering Hollywood, which was filled with beautiful women, nightlife, and entertainment, I hadn't succeeded in finding the girl of my dreams. Now, as a soldier, my major interest was to develop to my highest potential. My new goal was to continue adjusting to America, devote myself to military life, and swear off women. The latter goal, however, didn't last very long.

One Friday evening I noticed a young woman at the temple, and after services we were introduced because of our common German-Jewish background. Her name was Eva Rhee, and she taught Spanish and English at Salinas High School. I asked for her telephone number but informed her that I was busy reading Thomas Mann's fascinating *Magic Mountain* and would call her the following week if I finished the book by then. My comment must have sounded rather conceited, and she did not appreciate it.

Eva was born in Dortmund in Westphalia, Germany. When she was fourteen years old the Clarks, a wealthy Quaker family in England, saved her, her parents and her brother. The brother had been studying previously at Oxford and the Clarks invited Eva to go to high school in England. For one year the Rhees were houseguests of the Clarks, the owners of Clark Shoes, an international line. Eva's parents came to the U.S. in 1939 or 1940 and settled in Los Angeles. After graduating from Whittier College, a Quaker school, Eva became an English teacher. Lucky for me, after teaching for one year in Solvang, Eva moved to Salinas High School and became involved in the Salinas Jewish community.

Needless to say, I finished *Magic Mountain* and did call her. We made a date and she invited me to lunch the following weekend at her house in Alisal, the southern part of Salinas. I hitchhiked there to see her—about a 30-minute ride from Fort Ord. At that time a soldier in uniform could stand on the highway by the base and easily get picked up by people stopping to offer a ride. Today such a thing is impossible.

At Eva's house, I observed that the table was set with packaged cold cuts, Vienna sausages from a glass jar, a sleepy looking green salad, and store-bought cookies for dessert. Her menu was not much better than the army fare. Eva's cooking, clearly, did not match her intelligence, but I had not come primarily to eat. There were other redeeming features to the luncheon. As we sat by the fireside in her tiny living room, she and I discovered we had a lot in common besides being born in Germany.

We shared a love of classical music. Eva had no TV, but an old phonograph that entertained us with LP records, which had just come out and also 78-rpm records of chamber music by Mozart and symphonies by Beethoven and Schubert. We knew the same German poets and composers.

When Eva and I were growing up, Germany had either Liberal or Orthodox synagogues but no Conservative movement. Her family wasn't very religious but did belong to an Orthodox synagogue, where her father served on the board. My parents and I attended a synagogue that was actually similar to Conservative and was called Liberal and the prayers were mostly in Hebrew. Although the majority of German Jews were somewhat assimilated, they still observed major Jewish holidays.

Soon Eva and I were getting together every week. My English was improving by the day and Eva's reading to me from Kahlil Gibran's *The Prophet* gave me spiritual nourishment. Before long our friendship turned into a blossoming romance. One Sunday I offered to cook a gourmet meal for her and her landlady. She accepted gratefully, and my gesture—including chopped liver, filet mignon, and stuffed potatoes—made a lasting impression.

To get Eva to join me at services, I needed permission from the motor pool to carry civilian passengers. On Friday evenings, my army bus stopped regularly in front of her house. Once when an MP followed me, I had to do some explain why a civilian woman was riding on an army bus with 30 soldiers. The MP checked my trip ticket, smiled understandingly, and motioned me on. Eva was not usually a temple-goer, but she began attending every service. I'm not sure, though, that she actually came to pray.

Often Eva would fly to Los Angeles on weekends. To visit Eva in LA and her mother, I sometimes had to hitchhike, which often took two or three rides. In those days, people were often appreciative of servicemen, very friendly, and trusting. On one occasion a man picked me up and along the way he asked, "Do you have a driver's license?"

When I said yes, he admitted he was tired. "Would you mind driving to Santa Barbara while I nap?" he asked.

I agreed, he gave me the wheel, and when we reached his destination he invited me for lunch.

For Eva and me, Carmel-by-the-Sea was our favorite spot on earth. When spring arrived we explored the Monterey Peninsula on Sundays. Surrounded by nature, we hiked in Point Lobos State Park, strolled down Fisherman's Wharf, and visited Cannery Row, immortalized by John Steinbeck's novel of the same name. We picnicked on the beach, watched the waves, and basked in the sun. Six months went by and our relationship became even closer, but my time at Fort Ord was coming to an end.

One morning I received orders for a transfer to Fort Bragg, North Carolina. That meant having to say goodbye to Eva. We both were near tears. Thinking of parting, we stood motionless under the shade of the tall eucalyptus tree on the corner of Ocean and San Antonio Avenues in Carmel. This was the exact spot where I proposed to her. Being the cautious type, she said she had to think it over and would give me her answer in twenty-four hours. The answer came the next day and the rest, as they say, is history.

Oh, wondrous eucalyptus tree, pillar of our memory, you weathered many storms and have endured to this day. Every time I see you, I treasure the memories where Eva and I sealed our destiny. I recall,

> *More than fifty years ago*
> *I met my little diva.*
> *I really picked a winner,*
> *A true soul mate named Eva.*

## Chapter Twenty-Four

# Transfer to the South

My transfer to Fort Bragg, in June 1949, took me to a world unlike anything I had ever seen before.

I had watched the celebrated film "Gone with the Wind" and had read Mark Twain's *Tom Sawyer* and *Huckleberry Finn*. Yet meeting live Southerners and actually being in the South was quite different from movies and books. It was there I witnessed the first racial discrimination I saw in America.

Arriving by train at Fayetville, I was surprised that the railroad station was segregated. There were two restrooms and two water fountains, one for whites and one for "coloreds," as Blacks were called then. The "colored" fountain, I discovered, was not refrigerated. From the station I hopped on a city bus to get to my army post. At the next stop a black woman entered and I had another startling experience. She was very pregnant, looking as if she might give birth right there. I was sitting in the middle of the crowded bus and innocently, like a gentleman, I rose and offered her my seat.

The driver, observing me in his rearview mirror, turned around.

"You white trash!" he angrily yelled at me.

I was stunned.

But racial discrimination, I soon observed, occurred in the army too. Being stationed with my battalion was a dramatic learning experience. The military personnel were segregated and lived in special barracks. The African-Americans were assigned to designated areas and could not get jobs as doctors, teachers, waiters, or receptionists among others; they were the dishwashers, porters, domestics, and street cleaners. Their lot would begin to improve only after segregation was declared illegal in the late 1950s and when actions were taken by Dr. Martin Luther King Jr., the NAACP and the Urban League.

Aside from these disturbing facts about racial injustice, my life at Fort Bragg was a dream. I met wonderful people and was quick to make friends. A highlight was seeing President Harry Truman in person when he visited our base.

I was assigned to Special Services, a unit that gave me several different responsibilities. My job with Troop Information Program was to provide background on the latest world news to the battalion, whose attendance was compulsory. We didn't have a public radio or newspaper sources, but I received news bulletins from headquarters and prepared and delivered two 15-minute lectures a week. My accent apparently was not an issue because there were many other "foreigners" in the company from the Philippines and Mexico.

Since I was put in charge of the company recreation hall, I was trained to operate audiovisual equipment and became a projectionist. I also arranged for special activities like movies, maintained the ping pong and pool tables, and filled the Coke machine. The best part of my duty assignment, though, was having my own private room with a desk and a typewriter, which I used to write my daily love letters to Eva.

When the army chaplain, the military rabbi on our base, learned that I not only could lead Jewish services but was happy to be a volunteer cantor, he asked me to join him in officiating at different places like the Marine Base at Camp LeJune in Raleigh. During or after services, I often told stories about my background, a bit about Shanghai and also the Holocaust.

For my first High Holiday engagement I took the bus to Temple Beth El in Kinston. Temples always allowed military personnel to come in free, but that congregation consisted mostly of the Kinston Jewish community. Rabbi Tolotchko loved my chanting and like others before him, urged me to become a professional cantor after my discharge from the army. For the first time I received a small fee for my services.

Being in the army I had time to read and study so my military experience helped me grow intellectually. At the same time, my volunteer cantoring reinforced my spiritual attachment to Judaism and deepened my understanding that leading services is much more than just singing, that the spiritual aspect of a cantor's work is essential.

As busy and as happy as I was in North Carolina, though, I was most eager to get back to my beloved Eva to begin a new life together.

## Chapter Twenty-Five

# Embarrassing . . . or Not

Once there was a time in Europe when a prospective groom would ask for his bride's hand in marriage by appearing before her parents, sometimes getting down on his knees, and presenting his checkbook or some other evidence of his financial stability. When it was my time to meet my future mother-in-law and present the plans Eva and I had for our future, I appeared without even a savings book and only a few hundred dollars in my bank account.

As the saying goes, "money isn't everything," and in my case it was absolutely true. In 1949 I traveled to Los Angeles eager to make a good impression on Mrs. Else Rhee, Eva's mother. Even though Eva had come earlier to prepare her mother for the expected encounter, the meeting was a painful experience, as I had anticipated.

Mrs. Rhee was a refined and highly cultured lady from a well-to-do German-Jewish family. Her brother, Fritz Heinemann, a distinguished philosophy professor, taught at Oxford University. Mrs. Rhee herself was educated at Oxford, and her sister Lotti was a physician in Europe early in the 1900s, when it was quite unusual for women to become doctors.

Eva and her parents left Germany in 1939 to escape the Nazis. Max Rhee, Eva's father, was an amateur violinist and owner of a successful export business in Dortmund. He died soon after the family came to America and settled in Los Angeles. I was told that he was an unusual person, self-educated, and efficient. I felt he would have readily accepted me for we had a lot in common. Unfortunately, we could never meet.

Although the Rhee home was modest, it still reflected some old country glory. Because they had left Germany before World War II, they were able to bring many family heirlooms to England, where they were placed in storage and later shipped to America. Paintings by famous artists such as Chagall and

Kandinsky adorned the walls. Books by Goethe, Schiller, and Thomas Mann were prominently displayed. Mrs. Rhee was even able to save her Meissen china, Limoge porcelain, and the heavy, ornate silverware engraved with the family's initials.

Even before Mrs. Rhee met me, she disapproved of the relationship between Eva and myself. She had written Eva admonishing letters, urging her against our marriage. Exceedingly proud of her daughter's professional achievements, Mrs. Rhee imagined that a future son-in-law would have a similar educational background. A doctor or lawyer would have satisfied her and an accountant might also be considered acceptable. Being an intelligent, perceptive woman, Mrs. Rhee sized me up—sight unseen—as an uneducated, uncultured, happy-go-lucky soldier who also happened to be broke. She had high expectations for Eva's future husband, and in her eyes, I certainly did not measure up.

She was convinced that if Eva and I should have a family, we would surely starve. A cautious woman, she also evaluated my curriculum vitae with her friends and acquaintances prior to our meeting. None of them had ever met me, so of course I started out automatically with at least three strikes already against me.

"Why can't you wait a few years until you are well established?" Mrs. Rhee would ask. "To raise a family in your situation seems utterly irresponsible."

She even held my religious orientation against me by being critical.

"If you really have religious beliefs," she stated with authority, "then you would not involve my daughter in marriage without a sound financial basis."

I felt depressed and humiliated to be rejected by Mrs. Rhee. True, my on-paper resume was meager. After all, the Holocaust had deprived me of a higher education, and the death of my mother caused me to drop out of high school in Shanghai and go to work instead. During my military days my finances were rock bottom and all my worldly possessions fit into my army footlocker. Until now, my education and my teacher had been Life itself. Adversity had strengthened me and taught me the meaning and value of life, and I hoped that I would be respected for what I was.

Mrs. Rhee felt very close to her daughter, but Eva had a mind of her own. She knew me, was in love with me, and had faith in me.

"I must do what I want to do," she informed her disappointed mother. "And I *will* marry this man. *Period.*"

In spite of the negative input from her mother, the rest of Eva's family was much more accepting. In fact, Eva's uncle sent us a beautiful letter of approval.

"I think that young people should decide their own destiny and make their own life," he wrote, and he also enclosed the down payment for a new car.

On December 25, 1949, we had a simple wedding at the Chapman Park Hotel in Los Angeles. We served little canapés, cake, and punch and paid for it ourselves. From her girlfriend, Eva borrowed a wedding dress that fit perfectly. My baldheaded, potbellied Uncle Martin, an amateur pianist, provided musical accompaniment. Eva's brother Bob lives in Los Angeles. His wife, Irma, sang "*Ich liebe Dich*" by Beethoven. My father, still waiting to immigrate to America, was unable to attend because he was living in England at the time.

After the ceremony we drove to Lake Arrowhead for a honeymoon, taking advantage of Eva's winter break from school. As we left, no goodbye hug was forthcoming from Eva's mother. She just shook my hand coolly. Her parting words, unforgettable, still ring in my ears.

"Take good care of her," she admonished me.

# Chapteer Twenty-Six

# To Make a Good Marriage

Our honeymoon in Lake Arrowhead, a winter wonderland, was idyllic. We drove through the snowswept San Bernardino Mountains in our brand new Chevrolet. In those days every feature—like a radio or a heater—was "extra," so we bought the least expensive, stripped-down model. There was no air conditioning, a feature we certainly didn't need. Without a heater, we bundled up and sang to keep warm.

Trudging under the yellow pines powdered with newly fallen snow, we trekked around the frozen lake, skipped, and held hands as we contemplated our future life together, and spent five blissful days breathing the cool crisp air in the beauty of nature.

We were lucky to establish our new home in the most attractive area in America—the Monterey Peninsula—where we first met when I was a soldier at Fort Ord. We rented a small, cozy, furnished house in historic Monterey, California's first capitol. Carmel by the Sea, near the mouth of the Carmel River, with its scenic beach, sand dunes, and cypress trees was only a ten-minute drive from our house. Eva's favorite site was Point Lobos State Park, which faced the deep blue ocean and offered scenic coves, hiking trails and picnic facilities. And of course there was the world famous Pebble Beach with the Seventeen-Mile Drive, where I landed my new job after our wedding.

I had just completed one year of military service as a draftee and was ready to begin my five-year commitment in the reserve army; however, I was never called for reserve duty. During the two weeks prior to the wedding, I had busily set about finding a job and decided to apply for a position at the Del Monte Lodge. I was hired as chef of the Beach Club at Pebble Beach and made arrangements to start work after the honeymoon.

We had only one car, which I needed to get to and from work, so it was fortunate that Eva had her transportation taken care of. Every morning at 7:15 she was picked up by a colleague, a math teacher from Monterey who taught at the same high school in Salinas, and he brought her home at 5 P.M. About 8 P.M. I usually came home, happily, because Eva always greeted me with a kiss and often added romantic candlelight to our very simple meals.

"What's for dinner?" I would ask. "I made some spaghetti and meatballs. I hope that's okay!" she would often reply. Of course it was okay with me. I was so much in love it didn't matter what she served me. Sometimes, though, I did tease Eva about her culinary prowess, which left much to be desired. She didn't always appreciate my sense of humor, however, when I occasionally teasingly called her meals "burnt offerings."

The Better Homes and Gardens Cook Book that graced the kitchen shelf became Eva's bible for our eating fare. Her constant companions were products created by Betty Crocker, Aunt Jemima, Uncle Ben, and Chef Boyardee. Relying on her various measuring cups and a can opener, she strictly followed instructions on packages as well directions on recipes from her fellow teachers. The water for boiling a frozen vegetable was measured meticulously. If a level teaspoon of salt was called for, she used exactly a level teaspoon. If the cooking time was six minutes, Eva set a timer. She carefully followed instructions, no matter what. Sometimes I called her method "Eva's precision cookery."

The kitchen was simply not her forte and in those days we had no dishwasher. During our 50-year marriage, Eva never baked or stuffed a turkey. I didn't mind being headman and dishwasher at home because—aside from cooking—Eva possessed all the qualities a husband could possibly wish for. Her love was stronger than iron, and on top of that she was brilliant. She was greatly influenced by her Quaker education at Whittier College, which emphasized moral values, honesty, and helping others. She was an intellectual who was extremely modest. Her leadership inspired students to strive to reach the standards she set for educational excellence. Unsurpassed as a teacher, she also insisted on the correct use of the English language.

In the beginning I was always irked to be corrected when my syntax was out of whack. She let me have it when I said something like, "My wife and me were laying down for a nap." Needless to say both my spoken and written English miraculously improved almost overnight and so did my spelling, which was important, since computers and spell-check did not exist then. After a while I welcomed Eva's tutelage for she really meant well, and I became her favorite student. She accepted me with all my faults.

Eva handled our finances and balanced our checkbook to the penny. If it had been left to me, our gas, electricity, and telephone would have been disconnected long ago for lack of payment. Because she was an excellent correspondent, we maintained a lasting circle of friends. Eva was also extremely neat so her desk always looked orderly. In contrast, mine was messy, cluttered with stacks of letters, articles, and bills. Sometimes I couldn't even find my telephone when it rang.

After dinner, Eva sat down until midnight to correct tons of students' papers. Across the table from her, I was busy too—immersed in history books, studying to become a naturalized American citizen. I memorized perfectly the forty-eight states with their capitols. Hawaii and Alaska had not yet joined the Union then. I was able to name all the presidents from George Washington to the incumbent Harry S. Truman, and I could quote parts of the Constitution, the Bill of Rights, and the Gettysburg Address. I became familiar with the functions of our government's executive, legislative, and judicial branches.

Well prepared, I was examined on March 11, 1951 by a judge at the Salinas Superior Court. I passed, took the Oath of Allegiance, and proudly became an American citizen.

As a new citizen, I sent my father an affidavit for entry into the United States and brought him to Monterey from England. He had only a small amount of savings, so I helped support him and found him a job at Pebble Beach. After one year, though, he moved to San Francisco, where there was a German-Jewish community. He worked as a janitor at the Fairmont Hotel, which was owned by Benjamin Swig, a Jewish philanthropist who hired and helped many refugees.

About this time I happened to learn that Lucie Hartwich, one of my favorite teachers, also was living among other Shanghai ghetto survivors in the Bay Area. I located her phone number and eagerly called.

"Hi, Mrs. Hartwich! Here I am," I said.

"Hans Cohn! Are you following me?" she responded with elation.

I was delighted to make contact with her, an outstanding woman from my past. I had been her student in Berlin and Shanghai and will never forget her kindness after my mother died and I had to quit school. She was very proud of me when I told her I had become a chef, served in the U.S. army, was a citizen, and had just married. We were delighted to have discovered each other again.

Eva and I rarely went to movies, and we didn't own a television set, but we made our own music. I sang some Schubert songs and Eva accompanied me on the Bechstein grand piano. Her mother had brought the piano over from Germany and later gave it to us as a wedding present. Sometimes we invited friends for a musical evening. Our living room had a fireplace and often we sat without uttering a word, holding hands, watching the glowing embers slowly burn down as we drifted off to sleep. It was often after midnight by the time we staggered to bed, melting into each other's arms.

The nearest synagogue was located in Salinas. Sometimes we attended the Sabbath Eve services there and I volunteered as a cantor, helping Rabbi Stern by chanting the liturgy. There were not many Jewish residents on the Monterey Peninsula, so we began to invite a few Jewish families to our small living room for a home service, which I conducted. Since ten to twenty people regularly attended, we decided to form a small congregation and sought the guidance of Rabbis Paul Dublin and Henry Tavel, the two Jewish chaplains at Fort Ord.

Soon a religious school was established in our home and a number of children came once a week for Hebrew lessons. One of my first students was Ronald Levy, today a famous oncologist and a professor at Stanford University. The little congregation that was born in our house later became Congregation Beth Israel in Carmel, a well-established synagogue with a beautiful sanctuary, a permanent rabbi, and a membership of two hundred families.

Comfortably settled in Monterey, Eva and I began our new life with great enthusiasm. Although both fluent in the German language, for many years we refused to speak it, even in the intimacy of our own home. Eva told me of the intense fear and disgust she felt for the Nazis, and I shared her feelings.

We learned from each other with love and patience, understanding that the "We" in wedding comes before the "I." We loved our professions, the beautiful Monterey area, our community, and above all each other. And when our daughter Becki arrived nearly two years later—on September 9, 1952—we were a small but even happier family.

# FROM CHEF TO CANTOR

# Chapter Twenty-Seven

# An Impetuous Decision

While working four years as a chef at the exclusive Pebble Beach Lodge and Beach Club, Eva and I met many wonderful people who encouraged me to be on my own. So in 1953 I decided to go into business for myself, and we opened *Le Coq D'Or*, a cozy little restaurant and catering business on a side street in Carmel.

In the beginning it was hard. As the chef I was able to control expenses and not the number of customers. Often I gazed out the window of the restaurant's kitchen, wondering which passersby might be potential patrons. After a while, however, with my connections to Pebble Beach, the business soon blossomed, and many prominent families booked me for private parties. During these years, President Eisenhower came to Pebble Beach to play golf and Bing Crosby hosted an annual golf tournament. Such events helped me increase my clientele because they brought movie stars, celebrities, and internationally known golfers to the Monterey Peninsula.

Beef Stroganoff became one of the top *Le Coq D'Or* specialties. I even prepared a special low-calorie kosher version using non-dairy sour cream. I also introduced a takeout business so people could order casseroles featuring already cooked meals, which were an innovation at the time.

In 1955 when Eva became pregnant with Ruth, our second daughter, she took a leave from teaching, but continued taking care of all financial matters concerning the business. She was an excellent bookkeeper, which I certainly was not. I brought home all the receipts, she added them up and then paid the bills.

Things were going well for me, but I was working tirelessly, day and night. In my few spare moments I studied voice privately with Nancy Ness, a Norwegian opera singer who had retired in Carmel. On several occasions I was

engaged to sing a solo in local churches on Sunday mornings. At the annual
Carmel Bach Festival, I became a member of the chorus, doing small parts in
the concerts. In Bach's "Saint Matthew Passion," I sang the very small part
of Peter, who denied Christ twice. At the conductor's cue for my one-liner
part. I gave it all I had and sang out with gusto, *"I do not know the man!"*

At the end of the concert, a priest came up to compliment me.

"Mr. Cohn, I never heard a stronger denial!"

Becoming known as a young cantor, I was pleased to be invited several
times to officiate at High Holiday services at Congregation Beth Sholom in
San Francisco. Once again I began asking myself how I could realize my fer-
vent love for music and religion by becoming a full time professional—
instead of spending the rest of my life behind the stove in a hot kitchen, working long hours, and having little time left for my family.

After examining my life and my values, I understood that something was
missing; I urgently needed a greater sense of satisfaction and fulfillment. Situations beyond my control both in Berlin and Shanghai had deprived me of
an education, so I envied Eva, a university graduate and teacher. More and
more I found myself wishing to make a change and pursue my old childhood
dream of becoming a cantor.

The crucial moment of decision came one day while I was catering a party
during a golf tournament. I had spent hours preparing elegant salads and cold
dishes, decorating platters of scrumptious hors d'oeuvres with sprigs of pars-
ley and rosebud radishes, which I called the lipstick to my creations. The buffet I prepared was truly magnificent to behold. The thirsty guests arrived, consumed huge amounts of liquor, and began poking around in the food platters,
mindlessly mutilating the epicurean masterpieces I had so proudly created.

"Hans," a slightly inebriated guest demanded with a slur, "Bring me another Scotch and soda with a lemon twist—and very little ice!"

Depressed and offended by his and the other guests' indifference to my culinary expertise, it was suddenly very clear to me that I had, finally, *had it.* No
longer could I ignore the voice deep inside that was drawing me toward higher
aspirations, reminding me how, in my early years in Berlin, my religious faith
was strengthened by attending synagogue services with my parents. God had
given me a fine voice and I was, at last, determined to put it to good use.

The time was ripe for a change. Although financially successful in my
restaurant, I decided, at the age of thirty-one, to take a risk and make the sac-
rifice to begin a new career. Yet how, I wondered, could I do it, especially
since by then Eva was pregnant with our third child. Once again I recalled the
words I heard as a teenager in China when Major White told me, *Cohn, you
could sell rotten tomatoes.* Inspired to follow my passion, I talked to Eva. I
didn't have much selling to do because she already understood how I felt.

With her complete support, we sold the restaurant for a small profit, enough to keep us solvent for one year. After passing a battery of tests, I was accepted as a student at Hebrew Union College (HUC) in New York. With two small children, and a third due soon, Eva and I packed our belongings and in August 1957 moved east for what we knew would be five years of rigorous study.

We rented a little apartment facing Broadway in uptown Manhattan. Day and night trucks and buses roared by. What a change from peaceful, quiet Carmel with its pleasant, moderate weather. A car was financially out of our reach, so our mode of travel became public transportation.

Despite the many changes and adjustments, I felt content for the first time in my life. When I was admitted to HUC's School of Sacred Music, I grew spiritually and intellectually. Reading voraciously to make up for all the years I had missed, my life gained a new dimension as I became immersed in the study of modern Hebrew, music, philosophy, and history.

I was fortunate to be recommended to Alexander Kipnis, the world famous basso who taught voice at the Manhattan School of Music. I auditioned, and when he accepted me, another new world opened up. Eva and I purchased a used upright piano, white and antique, for one hundred dollars, and I began to take voice lessons. It was heaven to me.

The Big Apple, glamorous and exciting, with its skyscrapers and bustling cultural activities invited exploration. New York had so much to offer—the famous Metropolitan Opera, the New York Philharmonic, the Metropolitan Museum, and a variety of theaters on Broadway. Since our finances were quite limited, I bought standing-room tickets for three dollars to attend the opera and listen to the world's greatest voices. As a bass-baritone, my idols were George London, Cesare Siepe and especially Ezio Pinza, who was featured on Broadway in "South Pacific."

It was an exciting time to finally begin my cantorial studies, but I was concerned about my additional tasks. I chose to be optimistic because after all, where else in the world can one go to school full-time, work, and also support a family?

The old adage is true—Only in America!

# Chapter Twenty-Eight

# My Tuxedo

For Eva, adjusting to life in New York and taking care of our three daughters was a full-time job. For me, being a student was very time consuming, but I also needed to earn money. Good jobs, though, were hard to come by, especially part-time positions that would fit in with my class schedule at school. During my first year at Hebrew Union College, I worked at three different jobs and did most of my studying while traveling on subways.

On Sundays I taught Hebrew and Jewish history at a congregation in Croton-on-Hudson in New York. On Tuesday and Thursday afternoons, after my Seminary classes, I went straight to Westchester Reform Temple in Scarsdale, where I taught Hebrew. On Friday nights and Saturday mornings, I officiated as a student cantor at Shabbat services in Bayonne, New Jersey, a small synagogue that couldn't afford a full-time cantor. I was already familiar with leading services and the prayers and melodies I had learned in Shanghai came in very handy. In addition, I was also a "traveling cantor," substituting for other cantors who were ill or out of town.

Although the synagogue-related jobs helped support the family, they weren't quite enough. Since I was willing to do anything in the food line, I began my search by picking up a copy of the *New York Times* to examine the help-wanted ads. An interesting one caught my attention. "The Viennese Lantern," a prominent East Side restaurant, advertised:

**Wanted: Good driver to park cars, evenings,**
**Good benefits, Apply in person.**

Fascinated, I decided to apply for the position, but first stood outside in front of the restaurant, studying the menu displayed in the window. My mouth began to water as I noticed that two of my favorite foods were featured —

*Wiener Schnitzel* and *Apfelstrudel*. Entering the restaurant, I was immediately impressed by the succulent aroma of European cuisine that wafted through the dining room and filled my nostrils as I deeply inhaled.

Since I had just come from school to apply for the position, I was casually dressed. A waiter in a tuxedo approached and looked me up and down suspiciously.

"Can I help you?" he said with some disdain.

I asked to see the manager, instead, the owner himself came out to greet me. A well-fed gentleman with a big belly, he spoke with a thick Viennese accent.

His first question was, "Do you have a valid driver's license?"

"Yes," I said, then inquired about the benefits referred to in the ad.

"Well," he bellowed, "among other things, you may order anything you like on the menu, except liquor of course. You should know that our guests tip very generously!"

The job sounded inviting.

"By the way, where is your parking lot?" I asked.

"We don't have one," he said.

His answer surprised me.

"All you have to do," he continued nonchalantly, "is find a spot somewhere in the neighborhood and pick up the car when the guests have finished their meal."

I promised to let him know the next day whether I would accept his offer.

Upon leaving the restaurant, I began surveying the neighboring streets to look over the parking situation. After walking around for twenty-five minutes, I finally found one empty parking spot. Taking that job, I realized, meant I'd be lucky to park a maximum of four cars in one evening. There had to be an easier way to make a living, I decided, so the next day I thanked the owner and politely declined.

A few days later, I applied at the Waldorf Astoria Hotel and was hired as a *saucier* on the night shift, when I would be the sole kitchen person on duty, preparing room service requests from 6 P.M. to 2 A.M. At first it was interesting because some celebrities stayed at the Hotel. I made dishes for Cole Porter, a night owl who had a suite at the Waldorf and called room service when he entertained guests at very late hours.

The Waldorf experience lasted for only two weeks because being up most of the night and cooking over a hot stove took its toll on me. The next day, after getting barely four hours of sleep, I was exhausted and repeatedly dozed during my classes or while studying on the subway.

I needed to find work I could handle on top of being a student cantor and a Hebrew school teacher. One day I was fortunate to receive a personal recommendation to meet Mr. Roger Costamagna, a Frenchman who owned an exclusive catering business. He hired me as a waiter to help with private parties on evenings and weekends. A meticulous man, he prided himself on serving the finest epicurean cuisine. To present the food in a manner that did justice to his special clientele, he required his waiters to wear tuxedos, so I was forced to purchase one at Barney's, New York City's well-known clothier. I invested $57 on an outfit with all the necessary components including a tuxedo shirt, bow tie, and cummerbund.

The tuxedo purchase was one I never regretted although I did have one problem—what to do with it when I had to rush to a catering engagement directly from school. As a student I wore normal, everyday clothes so I sometimes carried the tuxedo with me to school, hidden away either in a suitcase or in a hanging bag. Wearing a tux during a class not only would have looked very strange, it would have also caused wear and tear on the garment. Most of the time I changed at the party site, but if the event was eight at night and school finished at three o'clock, I might go home first. I didn't do that often, though, because I felt ridiculous wearing a tux on the subway, which is how I traveled to work.

After being a chef for so many years, I was glad to be just a waiter. In fact, the less cooking I did the happier I was because working constantly in the kitchen around steam and smoke wasn't good for my vocal chords. Waiting on tables was not only better for my voice, though, it was also more profitable. Many of the parties we catered came through members of the United Nations and featured notable guests. It was a wonderful opportunity to meet distinguished people, to talk to them, and to see how the rich and famous lived. On one occasion I met the renowned violinist Mischa Elman.

On another memorable evening, we catered a diplomatic private party near Central Park at the exclusive, expensive Essex House, where wealthy residents hosted events. At that party Mr. Costamagna, noting that I was immaculately dressed in my brand new tuxedo, commented that I was a handsome young man, and he assigned me to take guests' wraps at the entrance door of the very luxurious apartment. A gentleman entered, greeted me cordially with a friendly smile, and shook my hand. I gladly obliged and returned his warm gesture.

Then I realized the man was Dr. Ralph Bunch, the well-known black attorney. As assistant to U.N. Secretary Dag Hamarskjold, Dr. Bunch served as mediator to the Arab-Israeli conflict and won the Nobel Peace Prize for helping establish the first cease-fire in 1949. In my new outfit I must have made an impression on him for he mistakenly assumed that I was the host of the party. After the mutual handshake, I said dutifully, "May I take your coat, Dr. Bunch?"

After working for two years with Mr. Costamagna, I had to leave that job because my cantorial and teaching responsibilities increased. To better suit my student hours, I took a position as an on-call cook with Patrician Caterers, a kosher company that prepared Bar and Bat Mitzvah and wedding parties at hotels when kosher cuisine was requested. Our venues included some of the finest New York sites—such as Hotel Pierre, the Astor House, and the Waldorf.

The Patrician owner, Mr. Goldman, recognized that in addition to my being a chef, I was also an excellent carver, so he put me in charge of a buffet section in the dining room where I sliced roast beef, prime rib, turkey, tongue, and brisket. At that time the pay was a mere $3.75 an hour, and I would go home with only fifteen dollars in my pocket after working like a dog during a hectic four-hour shift.

Disappointed, I approached Miss Levy, the catering manager.

"Look," I explained, "I can't possibly feed my wife and children on this meager salary."

She understood my dilemma and valued my skills and experience.

"Why don't you take home some leftover food?" she suggested. "We can't take it back or use it again anyway." As a kosher caterer, Patrician couldn't resell the food as strictly kosher because it might be unsupervised while being transferred from a kashered hotel kitchen to another locale. Miss Levy's suggestion delighted me.

From then on I came to work with a small suitcase, knowing it would later be filled with goodies. Sometimes Eva, the girls, and I had enough to eat for almost a whole week because I often brought home a hunk of roast beef, five pounds of chopped chicken liver, some turkey breast and a bag filled with dinner rolls. Often Eva waited up for me to sample the delicacies I had salvaged. The generous food leftovers compensated for my small paycheck, which no longer seemed so disappointing.

For years every time we looked inside my suitcase and noticed some traces of greasy spots, we fondly remembered Miss Levy. But I was always careful not to get any of those spots on my books.

## Chapter Twenty-Nine

# Catering and Cantoring

Summers in New York City are excruciatingly hot—often ninety or more degrees Fahrenheit with humidity to match. During my five years of study there, I kept my promise to Eva never to spend a summer in the city because she couldn't easily tolerate the heat. Coming from our ideal California climate, such conditions required quite an adjustment.

At the end of each school year, we looked forward to the twelve-week tourist season in the Catskill Mountains, which usually began on Memorial Day and continued through the Labor Day weekend. By our first New York summer, I was able to afford a car—a blue Chevrolet station wagon with whitewall tires but no air conditioning, a feature not yet available then. We loaded the children in the car and eagerly headed for the Catskills, also called the Borsht Belt or the Jewish Alps.

Borsht Belt history is rather unique. In the late 20s and early 30s, Jewish immigrants from Europe settled in the area, bought old structures or built cheap houses and began farming. An old Catskill joke tells of an enterprising visitor who crossbred a Guernsey with a Holstein and created a Goldstein. Some of these would-be farmers didn't succeed after discovering that the soil wasn't good for producing profitable crops and the growing season was too short. Many who failed at farming were disappointed financially and returned to the city.

Other immigrant newcomers, however, stayed on and began renting out rooms. Later they built bungalows to accommodate New York families who came up for an inexpensive vacation. After World War II, travel to Europe was not yet in vogue so the Catskills, being not far from the city, were a favorite, affordable vacation spot especially for New York Jews. Non-Jews also vacationed in the area, but their hotels were restricted and even advertised it.

For example, when hotels posted signs saying "Churches nearby," it was a code meant to keep Jews out. Such restrictions continued even into the 1950s.

Before long, in response to this discrimination, hundreds of Jewish hotels sprang up. Towns like Grossinger's, Fleischmanns, and Pine Hill were among the earliest. Some Jewish hotels offered summer camp for children, provided a synagogue on the premises, and served kosher cuisine. Three substantial meals and gluttony was the order of the day.

The drive to the Catskills took four hours, first on the New York thruway and then onto scenic Highway 28. Our destination was Fleischmanns, a resort town, and the Mathes Hotel, where I worked as a waiter. A second-rate hotel, the Mathes was not kosher but featured European Jewish-style cooking because Mr. Mathes, the owner and a German Jew, wanted to offer some Jewish traditions.

Every Friday we served challah prepared in the hotel bakery, homemade gefilte fish, and a complimentary glass of Mogen David wine. Mr. Mathes personally selected a lady guest to bless the Sabbath candles, and I sang the traditional *Kiddush* (the blessing over wine) and also led the assembled guests in "*Shalom Aleichem*," a popular Sabbath hymn. Dinner always included chicken soup and *tsimmes*, a type of beef and vegetable stew.

Although the Mathes Hotel didn't have regular services, it did have a Jewish atmosphere and tried to accommodate the guests. For example, if a guest had *yarhtzeit*—the anniversary of someone who died—and wanted a *minyan*, we made an announcement that ten men were needed after dinner, and I would lead a service for them to say the *Kaddish* prayer, recited in memory of the dead.

The Jewish clientele ate voraciously. They were not big drinkers. In fact, their two most popular pastimes were ravenous eating and basking in the sun by the swimming pool. In general, I found the hotel guests not as interesting as the other waiters, who were primarily law and medical students. Many guests were elderly folks who talked a lot about their aches, pains, and illnesses. A frequent comment or sort of inside joke was, "Be good to your waiter; he may be your doctor some day and take out your gallbladder!"

Eva and I rented a bungalow, a quaint little cottage nearby the Mathes. She and the children loved being surrounded by nature and breathing in fresh mountain air. Located in the foothills, Fleischmanns was near hiking trails, shady pine trees, and lots of blackberry bushes. Hotel guests were offered a weekly American plan rate with three full meals while our summer cottage came with a fully equipped kitchen in which the children, who loved to pick berries, would make pies.

At the Mathes, single waiters and chambermaids were paid just fifteen dollars a week including room and board, so they depended on their tips. Most of the help stayed in cheap accommodations, two or three to a room. My salary was also fifteen dollars a week for serving three meals a day to a station of forty guests. During the ten-week summer session I didn't have even one day off, but the tips made it well worthwhile. In addition, Mr. Mathes paid me an extra thirty-five dollars a week as a bartender and singer.

Directly after dinner I went to the bar and began making Martinis, Old Fashioneds, and other drinks I learned how to mix from studying a bartending book I purchased. In the evening, I performed three or so songs I had rehearsed earlier with a pianist after lunch. Accompanied by a small band— drum, piano, and saxophone—I sang tunes from musicals, Yiddish songs, and an occasional popular operatic aria like the "Toreador Song" from Carmen. I also imitated Al Jolson, my favorite singer, with songs like "April Showers," "Rock-a-bye Baby," and "You Made Me Love You."

A happy atmosphere prevailed and hotel employees not only mingled freely with the patrons, but in fact were often encouraged to do so. The owner would frequently grab me and insist, "Get out there, Hans, and dance with the guests!" Single women who came without a partner especially loved it. I was the only waiter who was married so I wasn't as enthusiastic about dancing with unattached women as some of the single waiters, who were looking for a good time. A few of my colleagues even met their future wives working in Catskills resorts. At night, stand-up comedians frequently entertained guests in the bar, and I especially remember the comedians Herbert Zernik and Eugene Hoffman, who were also in Shanghai during the war. I still recall many of their jokes. A lady greeted him in the hotel and said, "You look like my fourth husband." Zernik asked, "How many times have you been married, my dear?" She replied, "Three times!"

The bar closed at one o'clock in the morning, but since my bartending began immediately after dinner, I didn't have time to clear up my waiter's station and also prepare the tables for breakfast. Because I went to bed so late every night, Eva came to the hotel in the evening and set up my station for breakfast, which gave me a whole extra hour to sleep in the morning. She removed the soiled tablecloths from dinner, replaced them, and set up forty coffee cups, juice glasses, napkins, and sets of silverware.

At the Mathes each morning began with a sumptuous breakfast served in the dining room. I greeted the guests by rattling off the tremendous variety of items they could choose: all kinds of juices, omelets, herring, smoked white fish, rolls, eggs, meats, and all the different cereals that were available. Guests could eat all they wanted and they stuffed themselves to their hearts' content.

I vividly recall, though, how one fine day things abruptly changed. The dining room was half empty. Guests came in slowly, looking bedraggled and pale. I wondered what was wrong and started to take their orders in the usual fashion.

"And what you would like to begin with today?" I cheerfully asked. "Orange juice? pineapple? prune juice?" And I continued listing other items on the breakfast menu.

"Please . . . stop," mumbled my first guest with an expression of agony. "Please . . . just bring me some oatmeal . . . and toast."

I began to observe that there were two groups of guests in the dining room. The happier ones, I soon learned, had rooms with a private bath. The others were patrons with down-the-hall shared facilities which they sometimes didn't get to in time. Everyone, though, had diarrhea and stomach cramps.

"You too?" I heard guests whisper to each other. But what was the mysterious illness?

"We feed the help the same meals as our guests," Mr. Mathes came out to explain.

"And look at our waiters. They're fine. There must be something in the water supply."

I had my doubts about the owner's comments, so my detective mind began to work. Because I used to be a chef, it didn't take long to figure out what was wrong. The problem occurred at the previous night's dinner when we ran out of chopped liver, the featured appetizer. That's why the help didn't get any. I had noticed when I was in the kitchen that the chopped liver was stored in an aluminum pan. Clearly, the container had affected the paté, causing an unfortunate but mild case of food poisoning.

The hotel chef, of course, never divulged what really happened. Nor were the guests told the source of the problem. The chicken soup served later that day at dinner helped to cure the malaise. By the following morning, the health of our honored guests returned to normal, and it felt good to see smiling faces again.

That summer of 1960 the newspapers were filled with stories about the infamous U-2 reconnaissance plane that was forced down over Russia, capturing the pilot Francis Gary Powers. Whenever I think of that food poisoning situation, I remember how guests greeted each other, perhaps in jest, with a whispered, "You too?"

During our Catskills summers I spent nights with Eva and the family in the bungalow. Each afternoon I tried to rest there a bit and also spend some brief time with the girls. The bungalow next to ours was rented by Eva's friend, Marion. A wise, all-knowing woman, Marion religiously read the *Wall Street Journal* and was always giving us financial advice. She was greatly influenced by a sign she described: "*Jesus saves but Moses invests.*"

She would tell Eva, "Your husband works so hard. You really should let your money work for you."

Although it was never my goal to become a capitalist, at Fleischmanns I was impressed hearing success stories by guests who found shortcut ways to earn an income with other people's money, primarily in the stock market. So I was interested when one day Marion furnished Eva with a red-hot stock market tip: Cracker Barrel Markets, a small supermarket chain, was in financial straits. Marion reported that by good authority Korvette, a successful New York City discount store named after its founders (eight Jewish Korean War Veterans) planned to purchase Cracker Barrel Markets. The stock value, she assured us, would definitely double immediately after the transfer.

"Go for it!" she urged Eva and me. "It's a golden opportunity."

Since this was our very first investment, we called a stockbroker. Feeling a bit of both anticipation and apprehension, I took my hard-earned summer savings to buy forty shares of Cracker Barrel at $25 per share, for a total of one thousand dollars.

The following week we read in the financial page of the *New York Times* that the deal with Korvette fell through. Cracker Barrel was a red herring and went into Chapter Eleven. As the stock went way down, my blood pressure went way up, and my liquid assets took a nosedive. I sold our stock for the grand total of twenty-five cents a share. Thus, from an initial investment of one thousand dollars, I recouped a mere ten dollars. A novice in the world of finance, I learned then that buying stock is a risky business and when uninformed investors gamble on hot tips, they can lose money. Regrettably, I was one of those losers.

For my family's rented summer bungalow, I paid $600, and when each Catskills season ended, the generous tips plus salaries for being a waiter, a bartender, and a singer paid for my tuition, books, and voice lessons. We were never financially in arrears even while I was a student. In fact, we barely had to dig into our reserves from the sale of the Carmel restaurant in 1957. We led a frugal but contented life. Still, during the summer of 1960, the one thousand dollars I managed to save—and then lose—represented quite a lot of money.

Eva and the girls had a wonderful vacation, but by and large the summer was hard work for me. Even so, I didn't mind being exhausted because I was happy to have my family nearby, especially since some husbands who worked in the city could join their wives and children only on weekends.

Working fourteen hours a day and on into the night, I found the words of Dale Boughman quite apt for my situation.

> ". . . *It may be wise to make hay while the sun shines, but it is equally important to saw logs while the moon shines. . .*"

## Chapter Thirty

# A Dream Fulfilled

Looking back, I don't know how I ever managed to go to school, get top grades, work at several jobs, and also support my family. But the memory of those five previous, difficult years of work and study evaporated like a dream for one day on June 9, 1962. That day—my graduation from Hebrew Union College—was one of the happiest in Eva's and my life.

Most parents attend their children's graduation from college, but for me it was the other way around. Our three daughters, Becki, Ruth, and Barbara—in identical pink dresses with puffy sleeves and lace collars—attended the momentous occasion when I was ordained as a cantor and also received my Bachelor of Arts in Sacred Music.

The festive convocation was held at Temple Emmanuel on Fifth Avenue in New York City, the largest synagogue in the world. HUC's President Nelson Glueck, the famous archaeologist, officiated at the ceremony. Attired in my black robe and covered with a new prayer shawl embroidered at the neck with gold thread, I stood on the bimah as Dr. Glueck, laying his hands on my shoulders, bestowed on me the Priestly Blessing traditionally given to new members of the clergy.

> *"May the Lord bless you and guard you,*
> *May the Lord make His light to shine upon you*
> *And be gracious to you,*
> *May the Lord show you kindness and grant you peace."*

After graduation I found myself doing what I loved most—singing to God and leading others in prayer. My new profession gave me much satisfaction and, on top of it, I was being paid for my services. Who could ask for more? After auditioning for various congregational positions, I chose to be cantor and religious school principal of Temple Beth El in South Bend, Indiana.

We rented a spacious home on the outskirts of town, shipped our furniture from New York, and drove to our new, split-level house with a big back yard. We arrived shortly before the movers came with all our belongings, so the place was completely unfurnished. The owner met us, handed over the keys, and I opened the front door to inspect the spacious premises. Each girl was thrilled to have her own room—a big change from our cramped quarters in New York.

The many closets for storage especially delighted us. In the master bedroom I opened one closet and was stunned by what I saw. Nothing was in it except for a Nazi uniform on a hanger, complete with insignia and a swastika armband. A steel helmet lay on the floor next to a pair of army boots. I could not believe my eyes. Turning pale, I broke out into a cold sweat. My blood pressure rose and rose as a terror came over me.

"What did I get into?" I said aloud, my voice shaking and my heart pounding. Near tears, I confronted Eva. "We definitely can't move into this place," I announced. The movers had just arrived, but I stopped them from unpacking. We had to plan the next step.

Suddenly I recalled what I had heard about Indiana. Besides being the South Bend home of the "Fighting Irish" football team at the University of Notre Dame, the state was also notorious for its Ku-Klux-Klan activity. Klan groups began burning crosses after World War II when the U.S. Supreme Court outlawed compulsory segregation. The head of the Indiana Klan, D.C. Stephenson, was known for his dictatorial powers.

I visualized the house's owner, whom we had just met, in a white robe and hood. I wondered whether he knew we were Jewish. Cool-headed Eva calmed me down. She called the owner and he promptly came back to the house.

"Is anything wrong, Mrs. Cohn?" he inquired. He seemed to be a very pleasant man. When we took him to the closet, I asked, my voice still shaking, "What is it you left hanging here?"

"Oh," he said calmly, with a smile, "I took that off a dead Nazi during the war while we were fighting in France. It's a souvenir, and I forgot to take it with me when we moved out."

Eva and I breathed a sigh of relief, the movers resumed unloading the furniture, and we began to unpack—as if nothing had occurred.

Our next-door neighbors, the Wards, were Christians from Kentucky who had grown up with preconceived notions about Jews. We were the first they had ever met, and as we got to know each other, we became best of friends. Our daughter Barbara especially remembers the winters, when the neighbors froze their backyard and all the children went ice-skating and played together.

South Bend had three synagogues—Orthodox, Conservative, and Reform. Beth El, which had about 300 families, was affiliated with the American Reform Movement, founded in Cincinnati, Ohio. Initially I felt nervous being engaged both as cantor and principal of the religious school, but soon I became more concerned about several other things.

First, I discovered that Beth El was a leftwing Reform temple, and I felt uncomfortable with some of the synagogue's customs. Although it had discontinued its earlier practice of conducting Sabbath services on Sunday mornings, on Shabbat it did not hold regular services. Bar or Bat Mitzvahs took place on Friday nights. Shabbat services were held only when a Bar or Bat Mitzvah was scheduled. Otherwise, on Saturdays the rabbi came in to work on the synagogue bulletin, a practice which disturbed me greatly. For me, the Sabbath was designated as a day of rest.

The typical Beth El Friday night service itself took me a while to get used to. At my New York temple I was accustomed to wearing a *kipah* (skullcap). In fact, I had a very nice high, traditional cantor's hat, which was white for Yom Kippur. Rabbi Shulman, however, insisted on no head-covering at all. Being bareheaded in the synagogue felt strange because I was accustomed to having my head covered. I felt, subconsciously, rather topless. We also used the old Union Prayer Book, which was filled with English readings and prayers and had a minimum of Hebrew. The Union Hymnal, which supplemented the prayer book, made up much of the musical fare.

The temple had a wonderful pipe organ and an outstanding organist, Helen Bodine, whom we shared with the local Methodist church. Helen loved Jewish music and accompanied me when I sang classical cantorial pieces in Hebrew. Unfortunately, though, most of my solos were in English, so I purchased for myself an English copy of Schirmer's *52 Sacred Songs You Like To Sing*. The service was built around the rabbi's sermon, after which I offered solos from Mendelssohn's *Elijah*, such as "Lord God of Abraham," "It is Enough," or some lovely bass arias from Handel's oratorios. A favorite was "Arm, Arm Ye Brave" from *Judas Maccabeus*.

Rabbi Shulman, a staunch follower of the Classic Reform School, was a prophetic-looking figure—tall, imposing, with white hair and a sonorous speaking voice. Although thirty years my senior, he was quite formal and respectful to me in his demeanor. On Friday evenings he would say "Cantor, (he never called me by my first name) meet me at exactly two minutes to eight, robed, in front of my office. We will walk in together."

At precisely eight o'clock after the special organ prelude, the rabbi and I marched in like a wedding couple from the rear of the sanctuary as the congregation joined in the hymn:

> "*. . . Come O Sabbath Day and bring,*
> *Peace and healing in thy wing;*
> *And to every weary one*
> *Let God's word of blessing come:*
> *Thou shalt rest, thou shalt rest. . .*"

As we took our places on the pulpit, a woman from the congregation ascended to the podium, lit the Sabbath candles and read, "Come let us welcome the Sabbath. May its radiance illumine our hearts as we kindle these tapers." She then recited the traditional blessing, usually in an English transliteration from Hebrew, and then I sang it with the congregation.

For a Bar or Bat Mitzvah, only the girl or boy's parents were summoned to the bimah (Rabbi Shulman called it the *altar*) and honored with an *Aliyah* (being called up to the Torah). The service was fairly short, about an hour and a half, so the decorum was excellent and the congregation quite attentive. For the *Kaddish*, the memorial prayer for the departed, all worshipers stood up. This Reform custom appealed to me as no mourners were singled out.

At the end of the service, Rabbi Shulman stood in the center, resembling Aaron the High Priest with an outstretched arm, and intoned the final benediction: "May the Lord bless you and keep you." These words were the signal for the recessional and another hymn to accompany us as we proceeded to the social hall for the *Oneg Shabbat,* the refreshments following services. Sisterhood ladies sat at each end of the sweets-laden tables, ready to pour tea or coffee from a beautifully polished silver service. Bakers appointed from the membership brought their finest pastries, which were certainly hard to resist.

For two years before I came, the synagogue had no cantor. They instead hired Woody Hellenberg, a non-Jewish soloist whom they called 'cantor.' On holidays and special occasions a quartet of non-Jewish professional musicians sang. They could sightread a piece of music, perform it immediately, and sound very good. There was one problem, however. They butchered the Hebrew, which to me was more important than the notes. For example, instead of singing *mi-k'mo-cha*, they would say *mee-cha-moo-choo.* My job was to teach these professional singers how to pronounce the words. Even if only five people in the congregation know Hebrew, I believe they deserved to hear correct pronunciation.

I was particularly interested in working with Beth El's religious school, which had approximately 250 children ranging from kindergarten through tenth grade. The school's existing curriculum, I felt, needed to be embellished and become more traditional.

To encourage participation in our Sunday school and to make Friday night services more meaningful, I initiated a children's choir and hired a music teacher. She and I taught Jewish music and held a monthly family service. I introduced a short prayer assembly in the chapel to begin the Sunday School sessions, and the children sang the *Shema*, prayers, hymns, and Hebrew songs. It was a good way to get the parents, some of whom had two or three children in the school, to attend services.

My three girls went to South Bend public schools and also Beth El's religious school, so they were well integrated in both secular and Jewish settings. Since there was a shortage of teachers, I drafted my wife to teach Jewish social studies and holidays. Because their father was cantor and principal and their mother was teaching, the girls were somewhat self-conscious, feeling they had to be especially well behaved and they usually were. The Beth El congregation was warm and friendly to our whole family, so we all felt at home in South Bend.

To build up the Bar and Bat Mitzvah training, I began a new weekly Hebrew program, which initially caused some concern, because the principal of the South Bend Community Hebrew school (sponsored by the local Jewish Federation) saw my program as competition. After a few months I suggested to Beth El's president that we introduce regular Saturday morning Bar and Bat Mitzvahs. And eventually we did, after Rabbi Shulman approved my big innovation.

When no Bar Mitzvah was scheduled on a Shabbat morning, Saturday became my day off and I often attended the Orthodox William Street Synagogue, led by Rabbi Bergman. He welcomed me with open arms, invited me to participate, and I developed a cordial relationship both with him and his members. Out of respect for Orthodox tradition, the first time I drove there I parked several blocks away from the *Shul* (synagogue). Leaving services, though, I was surprised to see that half the congregants themselves drove away in cars that were parked right in front of the synagogue. Unlike Brooklyn or New York, where there's a *Shul* on every block, in South Bend people didn't walk to get to services especially during cold, snowy winters. The long distance would have made walking under those conditions a hardship or even hazardous.

Even in Berkeley, California—before I became a professional cantor—I was sensitive to Orthodox customs on Shabbat. In 1952 I was invited by Congregation Beth Israel to officiate for High Holidays, for which they then had neither rabbi nor cantor. They knew I wasn't Orthodox but even so I didn't like to drive up to the synagogue so I stayed in a nearby motel on University Avenue and walked.

I have many pleasant memories of my stay in South Bend. One occurred after religious school on a wintry Sunday. I was driving home in a miserable, cold snowstorm when I noticed ahead of me on the road a woman whose car had a flat tire. I got out to help, crawled under her car, removed the flat, and put on her spare tire. That was my mitzvah (good deed) for the day, I thought.

As I continued driving home, she seemed to be trailing me and I wondered why. I found out the next day when a beautiful bouquet of flowers was placed on our doorstep along with a note of appreciation from the woman. This experience convinced me yet again that there are many wonderful people in the world and I've been fortunate to have met quite a few.

A different kind of experience occurred on Friday, November 22, 1963, a date I'll never forget. That afternoon I was in my synagogue office planning a joyous service in honor of American Education Week. The Temple organist arrived to rehearse the music that I had selected to complement the rabbi's Shabbat sermon, entitled "Education Strengthens the Nation." Then the phone rang.

"Did you hear the news?" Eva asked in a tear-choked voice. "President Kennedy was assassinated . . . by a sniper bullet . . . in Dallas, Texas."

I was speechless and numb with disbelief.

Quickly we changed the planned program. Instead of the hymn "Rejoice in the Sabbath," I substituted "David's Lament" and the 23rd Psalm. Needless to say, our Temple was packed that evening with hundreds of grief-stricken congregants and also many non-Jews who flocked to the synagogue to share their horror about the young president's death.

Rabbi Shulman, a staunch Republican who was not very flexible, nevertheless stuck to his original sermon topic. The mournful congregation, flabbergasted, had to sit and listen to education-related problems. The rabbi's wife, Rose, sat in the front row almost dying from embarrassment.

To rectify the situation, the Temple Board put an ad in the local newspaper announcing a hastily planned memorial service. The following Sunday, a grim November day, congregants and friends gathered to share their sadness at the tragic death of our beloved president.

## Chapter Thirty-One

# Big Deal

While I was Cantor at Temple Beth El in South Bend, I applied to Notre Dame, a Catholic University, and was accepted in the master's degree program for Guidance and Counseling.

I was attracted to the Notre Dame program for several reasons. Because I frequently met with Temple people who faced difficulties, I was interested in learning strategies for counseling and problem solving as well as administration tips. Since I already had a principal's license from HUC, I wasn't required to take professional enrichment classes. But as administrator of Beth El's religious school, I worked with children so I wanted a stronger background in education and classroom management. I also wanted to keep up with some of my faculty who had advanced degrees.

The most important force that motivated me to apply to Notre Dame, however, was the fact that I was—and still am—a compulsive learner, always reading and trying to add to my knowledge. I cherish and believe in a Talmudic motto from *Ethics of the Fathers (Pirke Avot)*, which says, "He who does not add to his knowledge decreases it." I have found this true; forgetfulness diminishes our knowledge, so we must keep adding to it.

Academic classes at Catholic Notre Dame were quite a contrast from those at Hebrew Union College, where my classmates were rabbis and cantors. Being the only Jew in my classes at Notre Dame didn't faze me though because in New York I had previously taught a Comparative Religion course to my tenth-grade Confirmation class. Well aware of what to expect, I felt quite at home and accepted in a Catholic environment.

My new classmates were mostly nuns who had only recently been admitted into the program in the 1960s. Wanting to improve themselves, these ambitious women provided stiff competition. Since they were unmarried and didn't have much of a social life, they spent their nights in the library and worked until all hours studying, doing voluminous research, and producing extremely long and dense term papers. The exasperated professors pleaded with them to show mercy by writing shorter assignments.

"Sisters," the professors threatened, "if you submit term papers longer than sixty pages, we'll just have to stop reading."

Keeping up with these studious nuns was quite a challenge. I never worked so hard, but I held my own even though—unlike them—I went home to my family after classes. Some of the papers I wrote had to do with articulating my philosophy of education, devising a curriculum that ensures moral values, developing self-esteem and self-actualization, and practicing the theory of direct counseling with parents. I also had to prepare papers on statistics, a subject I found extremely boring.

In each classroom a large crucifix was displayed and every session began with students reverently reciting in unison the beautiful poetry of The Lord's Prayer. I had no qualms about joining in and in no time had the words memorized. The Lord's Prayer, sometimes called The Disciples' Prayer, asks for spiritual help, forgiveness, and physical healing. The prayer praises the greatness and majesty of the Almighty and yearns for the bringing about of His kingdom on earth. Such messianic ideals were taught by Jesus, the Jew, to his disciples, who were also Jewish.

The *Kaddish*, which means sanctification in Hebrew, is one of our oldest prayers. It is recited in memory of the dead, spoken in the Aramaic language, and is based on text from the Book of Daniel, 2:20. For more than 2000 years, since the days of the Second Temple in Jerusalem (586 BCE to 70 CE), the Kaddish has also been recited by rabbis in praise of God as they concluded a discourse on teaching Torah. Today the Kaddish, the most famous doxology in Judaism, is recited in every synagogue service. Both the words and the sentiments of the Kaddish share similarities with the Lord's Prayer.

The words of the Lord's Prayer include:

> "*. . . Our Father who art in heaven*
> *Hallowed be Thy name.*
> *Thy Kingdom come,*
> *Thy will be done. . ."*

The words of the Kaddish include:

> "*. . . May His great name be blessed forever and ever.*
> *Glorified and hallowed be His great name in the world,*
> *which he has created according to his will. May He establish*
> *His kingdom during your lives and the life of all Israel.*
> *Let us say: Amen. . ."*

The parallel between the two prayers is obvious, and that is why I had no problem joining my Catholic colleagues in recitation.

At Notre Dame, one of the great lessons I learned was that the more we study other faiths, the more likely we are to enhance our mutual understanding. I had good relations with my non-Jewish colleagues who were also enrolled in the Guidance and Counseling Program. Although there are some concepts that Judaism and Christianity do not share, we have in common many ethical and moral values that are universal. In the end, people are not very different from each other. By sharing our common aspirations, each of us can strive to make a better world through both words and deeds.

One universal maxim known to all humanity is, "Thou shall love thy neighbor as thyself." This sentiment from Leviticus (19:18) was interpreted by Hillel, a First Century Jewish rabbi, who chose different words. He said, "What is hateful to you, do not do to your neighbor." Similar ideas were also expressed by Confucius.

When my Beth El congregants learned I was studying at a Catholic university, they often asked, "Do you mind participating in The Lord's Prayer as a Jew at Notre Dame?"

"Of course not," my answer was always the same. "It's no big deal."

South Bend was a bridge and a stepping-stone in my career. As my first position, it was a valuable learning experience. Under Rabbi Shulman's guidance, we had an excellent religious school with a dedicated faculty. The rabbi's wife, Rose Shulman, from whom I took over as principal, was an outstanding educator, and I learned much from her.

Although Eva, the children, and I spent two happy years in South Bend and made many friends, we began to feel it was time to make a change. The Indiana climate was unpleasant with hot, humid summers and ice-cold winters. Eva missed California and for me, something else was missing. I preferred a more traditional Judaic practice than what was then available at Beth El. We could not refuse when an offer came from Rabbi David Teitelbaum of Temple Beth Jacob, a Conservative synagogue in Redwood City, California.

Coincidentally, Sheldon Merel, a Hebrew Union College classmate, was the first cantor at Beth El. I followed him in 1962. We both felt the Reform service at that time was too extreme. Over the years Reform services have become much more traditional, but my second professional position—in a Conservative synagogue—would become my permanent career.

Beth El hated to lose me because I did so much and introduced many new customs that were more traditional. But it was once again time to move on. I kept up with our South Bend friends, however, and even Rabbi Shulman, who visited me in Redwood City. In fact, I was still in touch with the Shulmans until not too long ago, when they both died, well into their nineties.

# MUSICAL MESSENGER

# Chapter Thirty-Two

# Return to the Golden State

With mixed feelings we left South Bend in July 1964, but the thought of returning to sunny California and to a new position at a more traditional synagogue was most alluring.

After acquiring another slightly used, low-mileage Chevrolet station wagon, we once again loaded our suitcases atop the baggage rack and placed a mattress in the back so Becki, Ruth, and Barbara would have a comfortable bed. Eva and I took turns at the wheel to keep from getting overtired.

Cars at that time still had no air conditioning so the summer heat affected all of us, especially the girls. In the car we played word games and sang songs, often with the children's repeated chorus lines from the rear: "Are we there yet, Daddy?" and "How much longer?" At the end of each day, we all looked forward to stopping overnight at a motel with a swimming pool. The girls could hardly wait to get into their bathing suits.

After being away from California for seven years, our journey felt like a homecoming, a road of joy and laughter after a long absence. It was thrilling to drive through vast open spaces, over mountains, verdant countryside, valleys, rippling fields, and healthy farm lands. We toured Colorado, visited the Mormon Tabernacle in Salt Lake City, and passed along the lonely Painted Desert Highway of Nevada. We encountered so much beauty in nature that sometimes we forgot the purpose of our trip—my beginning a new job in a new synagogue.

Leaving Reno, a dramatic change of scenery suddenly transformed the open road. It felt as though a curtain to an opera had opened when a sign appeared on the highway—"Welcome to California." I started singing my favorite Al Jolson ditty.

*". . . California, here I come, right back where I started from,*
*Where bowers of flowers bloom in the sun,*
*Each morning, at dawning, birdies sing and everything. . ."*

Entering the Tahoe National Forest, majestic redwoods greeted us along the Yuba River. After six days of glorious travel, we reached Hillsborough, California—our destination. There we drove to the home of the Goldstein family, longtime friends whom we knew before we left California. Since they were on a summer vacation in New York, they graciously made their beautiful house available to us for three weeks.

During that time we scouted around to find a house close to the temple. But Eva had another idea. As a schoolteacher, she focused on good education.

"Let's look first for a place with a fine school system," she suggested.

And we did. After some exploration, we chose Palo Alto, an academic community near Stanford University. A family-centered town with an excellent reputation, Palo Alto was an ideal place to bring up children. Near Mitchell Park we rented a small home with a fenced-in back where the girls could play.

"Look," Barbara called excitedly when the girls first saw the yard. "There's a real apricot tree!"

"And see the pretty flowers," chimed Ruth.

"Lemons! We have a lemon tree too!" Becki added.

In the summer the local Community Center offered outstanding athletic, music and theater programs for children. Besides, it was perfectly safe for the kids to walk or bike to school. Our new house made Eva so happy that I didn't mind having a twenty-minute commute to Redwood City, even though I sometimes made the trip twice a day.

By this time my mother-in-law's estimation of me had become more favorable. She saw that I worked hard and observed that I was respected and well liked. But Mrs. Rhee was not a warm person and my children never really got to know her. As a grandmother she never babysat for us, never kissed or hugged the children, and never had them sit on her lap. Despite her distant personality she was still proud of her grandchildren and bragged about them. She lived to the age of ninety.

A week after we settled in the house, I reported to Temple Beth Jacob, my new congregation. At that time the Temple was without a cantor, the religious school principal had quit, and Rabbi Teitlebaum was overburdened with organizational problems. Given those conditions, I was most cordially welcomed. In fact, the eagerly awaiting members greeted me with such enthusiasm, my arrival felt like the coming of the Messiah.

And so I began my long association with Beth Jacob and Rabbi Teitel-baum. For thirty-five years we served side by side in harmony, complement-ing each other. He, like Moses, was a teacher of Torah while I, like David, the sweet singer in the Bible, shared in the building of Jewish life through music with prayer and song.

## Chapter Thirty-Three

# A Case of Confusion

After beginning my tenure at Temple Beth Jacob in 1964, I applied for a Master's Degree at Stanford University in Palo Alto. Besides my natural zest for learning and a desire to improve myself, I also wanted to complete my Notre Dame studies, which were interrupted when we left South Bend for California. At Stanford, admissions were tight so I considered myself fortunate to be accepted in the School of Education.

As an educator with a love for children, I was always interested in the whole development and growth of individuals, so I enthusiastically registered for a required class taught by Dr. Oliver Byrd, a well-known physician. I was pleased that his Health Education 501 course was designed to harmonize physical well-being with sound mental health, both vital components in good all-around education. An old maxim still holds firm today—*mens sana in corpore sano*—a healthy mind in a healthy body.

Professor Byrd was an articulate lecturer who enjoyed a fine reputation. His own textbook on health was of vital interest to upcoming teachers. As a professor he was highly organized and I admired his outstanding, unusual methodology of instruction. It was when Professor Byrd took attendance that his greatest innovation occurred.

At the first session the forty registered students arrived promptly and quickly filled five rows of eight seats each. Then Dr. Byrd, with camera in hand, called students by name, asked them one by one to come up to the rostrum. Then he snapped a photo of every person. Although this procedure took quite a bit of class time, we all complied and also agreed to his request that we keep the same seats throughout the course.

Dr. Byrd quickly had his film processed and made a seating chart for himself by pasting the pictures in his roll book. By the second day of class the good professor was able to positively identify each of us. It felt good to be recognized immediately, and I was tremendously impressed when he called me and other students by name. An interesting incident, though, occurred with another student sitting near me. She was one of only two Japanese women in the class. When she raised her hand to ask a question, Dr. Byrd quickly acknowledged her.

"Yes, Mrs. Yamamoto?"

"I am sorry, sir, my name is Mrs. Takahashi," the woman responded, somewhat disappointed.

After a bit of embarrassment, the moment of confusion was quickly resolved. I found this incident both curious and beneficial because it gave me a better understanding of race relations. It was a reminder of how often we cannot distinguish many blacks or Asians because to us they look very much alike. Even Dr. Byrd fell into this trap since the only two students he mixed up were Japanese.

To get a degree in the School of Education, I had to take some boring busywork like statistics and the sociology of education. However, Dr. Byrd, who was very health conscious, designed his classes to be both useful and practical. While other professors assigned topics for their students' term papers, Dr. Byrd wanted his students to choose project meaningful for their own work. For my topic I selected medical concepts in the Hebrew Bible and mentioned various health issues such as cleanliness, keeping kosher, washing hands, and also salting meat to get rid of blood. I was happy because the project proved valuable in my teaching.

While other Stanford courses also helped me to be an effective teacher and educator, I particularly liked Dr. Byrd's approach, which stressed that as educators we teach more than a specific subject: we teach the child as a whole person. Along with the materials we impart to provide a good education, he reminded us how vital it is to be aware of a child's physical, emotional, and psychological stages of development.

His teaching method was unique and I was both impressed and influenced by it. I especially used certain of his instructional methods and strategies for classroom management. Later, when I had up to twenty students in my classes, I was able to very quickly memorize their names because I understood how important it was and how good it makes students (and anyone) feel to be called by name.

In schools today, technology is much superior to the old-fashioned methods that preceded the computer age. Although Dr. Byrd did use photo technology, he would have been an outstanding teacher even if he had used only chalk and a blackboard. When he retired, the department on health education—which he had created—was unfortunately discontinued.

## Chapter Thirty-Four

# The Many Faces of Being a Cantor

It was only after finally fulfilling my childhood dream of becoming a cantor that I realized just how many roles a cantorial career entails.

The cantor is the oldest religious functionary in Judaism. Traditionally called *hazzan* in Hebrew, the word means overseer and is of Assyrian origin. In ancient Israel, the hazzan was a teacher and also a custodian who handled synagogue affairs. According to the *Talmud* (a commentary of the Torah), the hazzan must possess specific qualities. He must be well-versed in the Scriptures, free from sin, humble, have a pleasing personality, possess a sweet voice, and, believe it or not, wear a beard—but not necessarily in that order.

In the Middle Ages, the hazzan was sometimes an itinerant singer, musician and poet, similar to the European minnesingers and minstrels. Later, the hazzan was called *cantor* from the Latin word for *singer*. Side by side with the rabbi, the cantor was indispensable in the synagogue and became a respected clergyman who led the congregation in prayer.

In my time, I have witnessed many changes in the cantorial world. When I started at Hebrew Union College in 1957 all the students were male. By 1990 women were admitted to the Cantors' Assembly for the first time. Reform and Conservative seminaries not only have accepted women rabbis and cantors but also have asked them to serve as National Cantorial Board members. These women have become an asset to the cantorate and I welcome their participation in the profession.

During the last thirty-five years at Temple Beth Jacob, I saw my career evolve into more complex roles as my functions became increasingly varied and demanding. In addition to being the cantor, I also headed the religious school since I had earned a principal's certificate after being trained in curriculum design as well as school administration.

Another new responsibility involved arranging teacher training sessions and workshops, in addition to the frequent and major challenge of finding qualified teachers willing to teach on a part-time basis. Also, as a faculty member of the Hebrew school, I taught Jewish music, provided classes in Hebrew, and prepared over a thousand children for Bar and Bat Mitzvah.

Even though Temple Beth Jacob had a capable director for our wonderful volunteer choir, Rhoda Keyson, it was nevertheless my duty to choose the music, arrange for programs, and attend weekly rehearsals. In our community I also performed numerous concerts and presented lectures on Jewish music.

On Sabbaths and festivals I read regularly from the Torah and also officiated at weddings, funerals, and other life cycle events. As Rabbi Teitelbaum's partner, I assisted him in his increasingly demanding duties, doing pastoral work, comforting the bereaved, and visiting the sick, either at home or in the hospital. Over the years, I laughed with our members on happy occasions and cried with them at times of sadness.

In my role as cantor and comforter, I often think of Arnie, a congregant whose story was an inspiration to me. Athletic, lean, and handsome, Arnie loved nature and the outdoors. Music was his avocation, and he especially loved Mozart. An avid reader, he devoured books. At thirty-two Arnie had his first heart attack, but with indomitable determination he bounced back to pursue his professional life as a prolific writer and editor for a computer company. His warm personality and delightful sense of humor made him beloved not only by his family but also by the many people he befriended.

At forty-three Arnie made the brave, major decision to have a heart transplant. Triumphing over difficult circumstances, he emerged resilient from surgery and determined to live his life with the best it had to offer. The new heart he received was truly a gift of life to be treasured and appreciated. Afterwards, he and his wife Eve traveled to England and hiked from coast to coast, enjoying nature and each other. Unfortunately, though, his longtime heart problem gradually exacerbated.

I remember the afternoon when a distraught Eve called to tell me that Arnie, then fifty-five, had just passed away. Active till his last moment, he succumbed to pneumonia and the end came quickly. Eve needed my assistance, so the following morning I went to her house in Palo Alto to plan a memorial service.

Sitting around the living room, we reminisced about Arnie's life. As Eve and her two daughters, Erica and Rebecca, further enlightened me about this remarkable man, their memories—between laughter and tears—were rekindled. Although saddened by their loss, which was not unexpected, Eve said, "We want the memorial to be a celebration of Arnie's life, to share the many happy years."

The Sabbath morning before Arnie's memorial service, we read in the synagogue a passage from the Book of Ezekiel (36:26), which was written 2,500 years ago. This expression of hope and faith had previously given Arnie and his wife a new beginning.

> "... *A new heart also will I give you,*
> *And a new spirit will I put within you.* . .*"*

I choose to remember Arnie not in the pain and hardship he endured, but as a warm blessing and inspiration, and I'm grateful that in one of my various cantorial roles I was able to offer needed support to his family.

> "... *We cannot, after all, judge a biography by the number of pages in it; We must judge by the richness of the contents. Sometimes the 'unfinished' are among the most beautiful symphonies.* . .*"*
>
> —*Victor Frankl*

My life as a cantor was demanding and stressful, often at the expense of neglecting my own family. Sometimes I would have welcomed a bed in my office. But the rewards far exceeded the demands.

> *The past is history,*
> *The future is a mystery,*
> *But the present is a gift.*

Each day *is* a gift and *music* too is a gift—a heavenly one. As a cantor, music became my vehicle of expression, transporting me with bliss and fulfillment. Although I am not a Pavarotti, I was always able to connect with my congregants. I have opened my soul to those willing to accept me in my synagogue. What comes from the heart touches the heart.

I find hope and relevance in my work and I have grown spiritually. I know where I belong and where I am going. Aesthetic beauty, the sound of music, and the silence of prayer and poetry uplift me. I steadfastly believe in God and I also believe there is still a lot of good in the world. I have received more than I have given, and in this spirit I am thankful.

> "... *Trust yourself; every heart vibrates to an iron string.* . .*"*
> —*Ralph Waldo Emerson*

## Chapter Thirty-Five

# From the Ashes

On Sunday, February 11, 1979 we held a memorial service to bury the charred Torahs in the courtyard of the temple. Seventeen rabbis and 1,500 people attended the solemn ceremony whose theme was "From the ashes rise Hope, Faith and Charity."

Rabbi Teitelbaum, talking into a bullhorn, told the crowd, "It is permitted to cry!" An eloquent speaker, he continued in a shaking, resolute voice, "Temple Beth Jacob will be rebuilt. They burned our Torahs, but they can't take away our faith."

As I chanted *El Male Rachamin*, a memorial prayer, I thought to myself how different America was from Germany in the 1930s. Here I felt surrounded by a wonderful, supportive community. The nightmarish tragedy that befell our synagogue actually brought us closer together. Our faith in humanity was bolstered by the sympathy and outrage expressed by the local community, which created the heartwarming Redwood City Cares Committee. Local churches and other synagogues offered us their facilities, so we didn't miss even one service.

Most of our activities and services in the first year were held in the nearby First Congregational Church. In the second year we often met at the Christian Temple of the Covenant, which had beautiful facilities and classrooms equipped with pianos. The neutral décor was plain and simple with no Christological symbols so our afternoon Hebrew School students were caused no discomfort.

Faith in restoring the synagogue was important yet it wasn't enough. Plans were on the drawing board to rebuild immediately since the structure of the building was still intact. But our insurance wasn't adequate to cover the cost, an estimated 1.5 million dollars. Much money had to be raised. News about the Beth Jacob fire received considerably publicity, and as a result of articles in the "Jerusalem Post" as well as other international publications, letters and contributions poured in from far and wide. Even so, these well-meaning donations weren't sufficient.

We all worried about where we would find the additional funds. To help out, I took on two new roles. First, I became a fundraiser. Many of my musician friends joined me and our choir to perform benefit concerts. In July, my vacation month, Eva and I went to Europe and thanks to friends in Cologne, I gave a concert in a cathedral in Moenchen-Glattbach, Germany.

It felt strange to see my name prominently displayed in store windows on posters advertising a Jewish concert in a German church. On the evening of the concert, I was warmly welcomed by a large crowd. When I performed a Hassidic medley with lots of bim-bams, I asked the audience to join me and I was overwhelmed by the enthusiasm of a mainly non-Jewish people singing along, clapping their hands, and sounding like a bunch of Hassidim. All concert proceeds were earmarked to Beth Jacob, so on coming home I proudly presented my congregation with a check for six hundred dollars, quite a handsome amount some twenty-five years ago.

Because we had no synagogue, I became an itinerant cantor, my second new role. I frequently traveled up and down to San Francisco and the Peninsula and often had to consult my book, checking my calendar to make sure I was in the right place. Most of our parents had no concern about their children attending Hebrew School in a church, but they did not want Bar or Bat Mitzvahs to take place there. As a result, we called other synagogues months ahead to inquire whether they had an opening available for us.

With one exception, every Bar or Bat Mitzvah was held in other synagogues. The Weintraub family insisted that their daughter Celisa's Bat Mitzvah be conducted in the burned-out shell of Temple Beth Jacob. We experienced an inspiring and unforgettable service sitting together in the unfinished, skeletal structure. Our Wednesday morning *minyans* (a required quorum for public worship) also met in the Temple's shell or in the parking lot.

Traveling to different locales for two-and-a-half years was a strain, but I held up very well and also endeared myself to our members and the community at large. Although during my years in New York I never had the opportunity to appear on Broadway, I made my first stage appearance at the Fox Theater on Broadway in Redwood City—conducting High Holy Day services.

At the end of summer in 1981, Temple Beth Jacob—like a phoenix rising from the ashes—was rededicated and we were at last back home in our own facility. Fred Gilman, Beth Jacob's new president then, worked tirelessly on the rebuilding. Rabbi Teitelbaum, our dedicated leader, gave an inspiring "coming home" sermon, alluding to the ancient Jerusalem temple built by

King Solomon and destroyed by the Babylonians. The Rabbi and I were surrounded by colleagues who came to wish us well, including the mayor of Redwood City and other dignitaries. Standing side by side on the bimah, as we had done in the past, he and I led the congregation in prayers.

Many generous donors contributed toward our newly restored synagogue, which included a rebuilt sanctuary, a new social hall, and a brand new chapel intended for informal services as well as for our weekly junior congregation. In the main sanctuary, gifts provided for an upright piano, new paneling, curtains for the ark, a pulpit table for reading the Torah, and an eternal light. The Jewish Theological Seminary sent us a new Torah to replace the one destroyed in the fire.

I was thrilled to be back in my rebuilt office along with my books and music, which had been spared by the fire and safely stored in my garage during the reconstruction.

It was disappointing, though, that no one was found guilty of setting the three-alarm blaze. Arson was clearly the cause because it was otherwise incomprehensible how flames could have sped so quickly from one end of the building to the other. The FBI was called in to investigate, but apparently there were no clues. No chemical substances were discovered or problems with the electrical system, yet flammable liquid must have been methodically set out to create such a fierce blaze. No one was ever charged or arrested, which left me with an uneasy feeling.

Although it was less than satisfying, the FBI concluded that the mysterious fire was one of "undetermined origin."

## Chapter Thirty-Six

# The Debate That Saved a Community

*Who is wise?*
*He who learns from everyone.*
*——The Talmud*

This Talmudic dictum, which has greatly influenced me as a teacher, has been a guiding watchword in my educational development because I have learned so much both from my students as well as my teachers.

Early in my career I was also influenced by a teacher I met at a conference on Jewish education in New York. Peninah Schram, a professor of Speech and Drama at Yeshiva University, was a remarkable lady who expanded my outlook on teaching and helped me become a more effective communicator.

Lots of people can tell or read stories. Some, though, can put an audience to sleep even when reading great literature. Others, like Peninah Schram, are able to engage listeners by reciting something as pedestrian as the Greyhound bus schedule. An exceptional teacher and reader, Prof. Schram presented a storytelling workshop that changed my life. I sat spellbound. Listening to her soft-spoken voice, her choice of words, inflections and gestures, I found myself involved emotionally, transfigured into another world. If she told a tale that involved food, I could smell it. If she described something, I could see it.

A teacher standing in front of a class is partly putting on a show in order to motivate the kids. Peninah taught us effective ways to make educational use of stories—to memorize parts, act out parts, and maintain eye contact. Inspired by her, I added storytelling as a new medium to transmit Judaism, in addition to using my guitar for songs and prayers. I collected more tales, as well as jokes and took advantage of the dramatic ability that I learned as a singer. Such techniques, combined with music, are wonderful media that spice up classes and capture the interest of young people.

"Telling stories gives children a storehouse of memories from which to draw the values of our people," Peninah said. She showed us that the Torah contains stories that transmit moral values still relevant today as well as ethical concepts that will never be outmoded, such as "Love your neighbor as yourself" and "Don't stand idly by while your brother's blood is shed."

As a result of Peninah's wisdom, I was often greeted when entering my classroom by, "Cantor, will you tell us a new story today?" Frequently I would relate an experience from my own colorful life, which the kids loved to hear about. Even today I meet former students, now married, who tell me they still remember some of my stories.

Teaching in an afternoon synagogue school requires ingenuity and careful preparation, especially because the children have already spent six to seven hours in public school. When I had a tale or legend to tell, I more or less built my teaching around it so the students would find the message more interesting. That methodology worked. Along with my story collection, music and prayer was a powerful vehicle that evoked good feelings, and I was able to inculcate my objectives without discipline problems and without boring the students. By having a variety of short sessions, they had no time to fool around since I kept them busy playing games, reading to them, singing, and even teaching folk dancing.

I also employed something I had picked up in South Bend from Rabbi Bergman. When we marched around with the Torah during the adult services, he passed around candy (he kept chocolate bars on the bimah), which helped attract the children to attend services. When I became Cantor at Beth Jacob, I bought a box of forty-eight candy bars and made myself very popular. Today Rabbi Ezray, who became Beth Jacob's leader after Rabbi Teitelbaum retired, continues that same tradition. Every month children come into the main service and the rabbi, instead of delivering a sermon, gives the children a quiz about the Torah portion. Then he gives out candy as a reward. So he too indirectly inherited something from Rabbi Bergman.

It's true that I wielded a powerful weapon, having authority to determine whether my students were prepared for Bar or Bat Mitzvah, yet I never had a problem with kids hating Hebrew school. In fact, an annual highlight for my classes was coming to my house for *Sukkot*, a Jewish harvest holiday, building a *Sukkah* (a hut), and then eating a festive meal there together. The kids loved to come to my class.

Twice a week I taught a two-hour class that included *trope* (a form of Bible cantillation), music, and the Holocaust. Although the Nazi period was the saddest in our history, I understood that if one teaches Jewish history only as anti-Semitism and persecution, the kids get depressed. They wonder—why bother to be Jewish? I tried to balance the tragic events with funny episodes to keep the students engaged.

I emphasized the joy of being Jewish, which always must be stressed in order to engender a positive feeling of identity and a pride of belonging. In Jewish history there are many happy occasions like Purim and Chanukah, as well as times when Jews enjoyed success and made outstanding contributions in medicine, science, agriculture and many other fields.

As a teacher I have observed how people can interpret the same information differently. The Mercedes logo—"Perception is not always Reality"—supports the idea that what one person considers a fact may just be an opinion according to someone else. I don't know how true the following tale is, but it's a good example of how sadness for one individual can be transformed into something more positive for another.

The story supposedly takes place in the Jewish community of Constantinople (today's Istanbul), which we do know was often the target of persecution. During the reign of Pope Leo III (721–722), an edict was issued for Jews to either leave the city or be baptized. To confront this dilemma, which threatened the community's existence, the frightened Jewish leaders gathered. After much discussion, they decided to send a representative to intercede on their behalf and chose Reb Daniel to propose a debate with the Pope.

When the papal office was contacted regarding this matter, the Pope was indignant. "A debate?" he gasped, "That's preposterous! I am the Pope. I shall not debate."

After Reb Daniel continued to implore, however, the Pope eventually agreed to a one-hour debate. "But," he demanded, "there's one condition. No words can be uttered."

On the designated day the Pope entered his chamber, raised his right hand, and put up three fingers. Reb Daniel then lifted his right hand and displayed one finger. The Pope seemed curious and continued by encircling his head with his finger.

At that, Reb Daniel pointed his finger to the ground. The Pope, appearing surprised, took out wine and wafers. When Reb Daniel dug into his pocket and brought out an apple, the Pope stomped out of his chamber in a rage.

"Why did you give up so soon?" asked his astonished assistant.

"I raised three fingers for the Trinity," the furious Pope explained. "And what did that Jewish representative do? He raised one finger to show we are all one. Then I circled my head to display the holiness of the divinity, but he pointed to the ground, telling me we are all anchored to the earth. Finally, I brought out the wine and wafers for the Eucharist, and he took out an apple, reminding me of the Garden of Eden."

"The debate is over," sighed the humiliated Pope. "That Jewish representative is just too smart for me." And he cancelled the Edict of Expulsion.

Reb Daniel, utterly bewildered, left the Pope's chamber and returned to his jubilant community, which greeted him with a barrage of questions.

"How did you win?" they asked. "Tell us what happened!"

"I don't know," replied the puzzled representative. "The Pope raised three fingers, signifying that we have only three days to leave Constantinople. I held up one finger to mean he could at least give us one week. Then the Pope circled his head to say that he had us surrounded, so I pointed to the ground, to tell him we're staying right here. After that the Pope took out his lunch, so I took out mine."

This amusing legend shows not only how easily misinterpretations and misunderstandings can occur, but also how sometimes differing perceptions may prove to be a saving grace.

## Chapter Thirty-Seven

# Tales of Character

Overlooking Jerusalem on the Hill of Remembrance stands the Martyrs and Heroes Memorial to the victims of the Holocaust. In Hebrew the hill is called *Har Hazikaron* and the Memorial is called *Yad Vashem*, an ancient name first mentioned in Isaiah 56:5.

In 1983 Eva and I stood together on that hill, commenting that although nearly thirty-eight years had then passed since the end of the World War II, people were still discovering information, artifacts, and evidence of the atrocities and horrors perpetrated by the Nazis. Those who survived and witnessed the Holocaust are dying out and their testimonies are being replaced by archives and memorials.

The whole story will probably never be told. A quotation by Shakespeare's *Julius Caesar* came to mind:

> ". . . *The evil that men do lives after them,*
> *The good is oft interred with their bones. . ."*

The interior of *Yad VaShem* is a shrine containing an eternal flame that is surrounded by names of the extermination camps inscribed on the floor. Outside *Yad VaShem* is a beautiful garden and a tree-lined street called Avenue of the Righteous. Trees here are planted with markers honoring some of the non-Jews who risked their lives to hide or save Jews from the Nazi murderers. There are also countless other righteous gentiles remembered who were not memorialized with a tree.

Thinking of such personalities, I am reminded of many outstanding non-Jews. Max Schmeling, for instance, was the German world heavyweight champion. In 1936 he became a national hero after defeating Joe Louis, who was black. But in 1938, when I was twelve, Schmeling was knocked out by

134

Joe Louis in the first round of a return bout. By losing to Louis, and also by refusing to fire his Jewish manager, Schmeling incurred the wrath of Hitler, who from then on snubbed the ex-champion.

Today, Joe Louis is well remembered in America, while Max Schmeling is almost forgotten. Yet, during Kristallnacht in November 1938 Schmeling hid two Jewish boys from the Nazis—Henry and Werner Lewin. In 1989 at the age of eighty-four, he was honored by one of the boys whose life he saved—Henry Lewin, president of the Hilton Hotel in Las Vegas. Today, sixty years later, a Berlin sports arena was dedicated in his name. Max Schmeling died in February 2005 at the age of ninety-nine.

In Krakow, Poland in 1939 Oscar Schindler heard Yitzhak Stern, his Jewish accountant, quote the following verse from the *Talmud*, a commentary on the Bible.

> ". . . *He who saves one life,*
> *It is as though*
> *He saved the entire world. . .*"

Schindler, impressed by that quotation, never forgot it. In fact, he made it his mission to save hundreds of persecuted Jews.

Raoul Wallenberg, a Swedish diplomat, risked his life to save thousands of Jews in Hungary from deportation. Sempo Sughihara, the Japanese consul in Kovno, Lithuania, was dismissed from his office after he issued transit visas to thousands of Jews, thus allowing them to get to Shanghai via Japan.

Joop Westerwill, a Righteous Gentile from Holland, was posthumously honored. A dockworker with a compelling sense of morals and justice, Joop smuggled hundreds of children from Holland to France and Spain, using his own money. In March 1944 he was captured by the Nazis and executed.

When tiny Denmark fell under Nazi occupation in 1940, the German invaders ordered the Danish government to round up all Jews for transport to extermination camps. However, a Danish underground organization called "Elsinore Sewing Club" arranged a clandestine escape for the entire Jewish population of eight thousand. By using a secret route through Elsinore, a waterway separating Denmark from Sweden, the "Sewing Club" ferried the Danish Jews to Sweden.

My greatest admiration, though, goes to Bulgarian leaders. Only recently, I learned that due to the heroism of King Boris III and the Orthodox Bulgarian Patriarch, the Church in 1943 resisted the forceful deportation of Bulgarian Jews and saved fifty-three thousand Jewish citizens. The true story of this remarkable rescue became known only after the 1991 defeat of the Bulgarian Communists, who had suppressed the story of the country's heroism.

Many people are unaware of these tales of heroism and many other similar courageous stories.

When Hitler came to power, both Eva and I were children. Her parents had a comfortable home in the city of Dortmund, Westphalia and her best friend was Gicka, a non-Jewish girl who lived next door. Inseparable, the two met every day via an opening in the fence between their houses. Something suddenly changed, though, after Gicka joined the Hitler Youth. One morning when Eva rang the bell at Gicka's house, the door was slammed in her face. Terribly upset and shaken, Eva came home crying. A beautiful relationship was ended. Unfortunately, the majority of Germans acted in a similar fashion.

A few years after the war, Eva was quite surprised one day to receive an envelope from Germany containing a letter from Gicka.

> "*. . . Dear Eva,*
>
> *You may not want to read on after the way I treated you, but I had to let you know how terrible I felt when you came to our door to play with me. The incident has haunted me all my life. Forgiveness, if that is possible, would lighten the pain and guilt I endured all these years. . ."*

We assumed Gicka had found our address by contacting Eva's childhood nanny, with whom we had stayed in contact and visited during our previous trips to Germany. Some time later, during a subsequent trip to Dortmund we visited Gicka and met her family. A happy reunion ensued as we sat in her house, shared coffee with *Apfelkuchen*, and talked about old times. Eva didn't harbor any ill feelings or blame her friend for what she did. A few months after our visit, Gicka succumbed to breast cancer. When her husband informed us of Gicka's death, he mentioned how relieved she was to connect again with Eva.

The story of Anne Frank has become an inspiring epic in the chronicles of Jewish history. She perished in the Bergen Belsen Concentration Camp shortly before the war ended. In her diary she wrote,

> "*. . . It is really a wonder that I haven't dropped my ideals, because they seem to be too absurd to carry out. Yet I keep them because of everything I still believe. People are good at heart. . . If I look into the heavens, I think that it will all come out right one of these days, that the cruelty will end, and peace and tranquility will return again. . ."*

Hitler and his oligarchy represent the epitome of evil, unprecedented in human history. There are many questions about how the world reacted to this tragedy and whether it could have been avoided, but there are few answers. Nevertheless, what remains today is to teach the Holocaust to future generations, keeping alive the memory of those innocent millions who perished.

## Chapter Thirty-Eight

# A Bridge of Understanding

In the Jewish calendar the Sabbath of Sabbaths is *Yom Kippur*, the Day of Atonement. This solemn holy day is designated for remembering, forgiving, and beginning anew. The spirit of forgiveness, however, does not come easily to a people whose history is filled with stories of persecution. Today the memorial services on Yom Kippur that recall the names of the departed include the Jews murdered by the Nazis during the Holocaust, Jews and Israelis killed by Arab terrorists, and all other lost loved ones.

Responding to the dilemma of how to forgive, but also how not to forget, I participated in the creation of a unique project. It all began in August 1986 when Eva and I were in Bonn, Germany having a cozy dinner with a non-Jewish German friend, Professor Hans Adolf Jacobsen and his wife, Dorette. Hans Adolf was director of the Institute of Political Science at the University of Bonn. Over the years he had lectured in the United States, addressed many different groups, and always identified with Jews and their tragic experiences in Hitler's Germany.

As we enjoyed dessert and coffee, Hans Adolf turned to me and said, "I have a dream, and I wonder if you could help me make it come true."

"Certainly, if I can," I replied, curious about what he had in mind.

"It's my idea," he confided, "to bring together members of the American Jewish Community—especially the younger generation—with the young people of Germany."

For a few moments I didn't respond. I recalled that during his previous visits to America he encountered a strong resentment toward Germans especially among Jewish people. I understood what he had experienced since members of my own congregation, mainly the older generation, had criticized me whenever I visited Germany and sang in various synagogues there.

137

"*You're* going to Germany? That country of murderers?" some chastised. Others demanded, "How can a Jew—who was born in Berlin and thrown out of Germany—set foot in that land after what happened there?" Others scorned, "In spite of the Nazi atrocities you *still* want to go there?"

Speaking intently, Hans Adolf continued, "I believe the time has come to build a bridge of understanding, so others can see the changes in today's democratic Germany."

I agreed that he had a generally good idea. In fact, after several visits to Germany, I myself had concluded that the time was ripe for such a project. After pausing a moment, Hans Adolf asked me directly, "Can you get together a group of Jewish students to meet with young Germans for a dialogue and an open exchange?"

His question prompted me to consider what I knew about young American Jews, most of whom were two generations removed from the Holocaust. I wondered whether they had something to learn from that history or whether they could possibly forgive the Nazi crimes.

"I'll do my best," I told him.

Upon returning to California I contacted Hillel, the Jewish student organization at Stanford and its rabbi, Ari Cartun, to discuss plans for such a trip.

Several issues concerned me. Fifty years had passed since the infamous *Kristallnacht,* the Night of Broken Glass, when all the synagogues in Germany and Austria were burned down. Also, I was quite aware that the young German generation doesn't feel guilty about the past, and they shouldn't. After all, they were not even born during those terrible atrocities. Besides, Jewish tradition teaches us not to hold children responsible for the sins of their fathers.

Yet, although the wounds of the past were perhaps beginning to heal, forgiving the horrible Nazi persecution seemed most difficult. Even though more current horrible wars, terrorism, and mass murders continue unabated in Israel, the Middle East, Africa, and other parts of the world, *nothing* can compare to the Nazi-perpetrated Holocaust.

In spite of some reservations, I knew it would be beneficial for German and Jewish young people to meet in person and get to know each other through conversation and personal interaction. The Stanford students who were interested came with apprehension and fear, not knowing what to expect. Some were children of Holocaust survivors, who joined the trip much against the will of their parents.

For example, at the San Francisco airport where we checked in with Lufthansa Airlines, one student didn't have her ticket and passport in order, so the clerk at the counter gave her a hard time. Immediately the girl's mother, standing nearby, remarked to her daughter, "You see? What did I tell you? Anti-Semitism is already starting here, and you haven't even left yet."

Our trip was sponsored by the German Foreign Office, which is comparable to our State Department. The group arrived in the beautiful city of Bonn, then the capital of West Germany. You wondered how such barbarism could happen in so civilized a country, but it did. We were housed in private homes with families arranged by the *Gesellschaft fuer Juedische und Christliche Zusammenarbeit*—Society for Cooperation of Christians and Jews. Our friendly and accommodating hosts made every effort to make us heartily welcome.

We met the *Bundeskanzler*, Chancellor Helmut Kohl, while the Christian Democratic Union (CDU) was in power. Other invitations came from the Socialist Party (SPD) and the Green Party. We had to meet these representatives separately because they refused to sit at the same table together.

We learned about changes that had taken place in Germany and that anti-Semitism was now against the law. It does exist there, of course, but anti-Semitism also exists all over the world. Germany has a small Neo-Nazi Party, which is illegal, but we were told that the Nazi paraphernalia sold in Germany comes from Lincoln, Nebraska, since producing such material in Germany is prohibited by law.

The German Press Club invited our group to an elegant luncheon where the editor of *Die Zeit*, one of Germany's leading newspapers, addressed us. The German Federal Republic, he said, is now a true democracy for the first time. We visited Mr. Ben Ari, the Israeli Consul General, who told us that the Israeli Consulate is the best-guarded building in Bonn. Next to the United States, he said, Germany is Israel's best friend.

As guests of the Federal Department of Education, we perused textbooks and were assured that the Holocaust is now included in the curriculum of all German schools. Until recently, though, the tragedy of the Holocaust had been swept under the rug. The docudrama "Holocaust," shown on television in Germany and the movie "Schindler's List" later helped to bring about some changes. An encounter with German high school students was the highlight of our trip. Being fluent in German, I acted as interpreter and asked the students, "How many famous Jews can you name?"

Their answers were surprising and disappointing. Mendelssohn and Einstein were the only names they could come up with. The students discussed the Middle East and were not embarrassed to express criticism of Israel's presence in disputed lands. The German students also brought up America's treatment of Blacks.

Not every attempt at Jewish-German reconciliation proved totally successful. At the German high school we encountered undercurrents of prejudice from students who resented that they had to pay restitution for what their grandparents did fifty years earlier. One student remarked that he felt somewhat saturated hearing so much about the Holocaust.

But in general these young people were now willing to accept the Holocaust and face the terrible atrocities the Nazis inflicted on the Jews. We also met two young Germans who had visited Israel and even worked as volunteers on a kibbutz.

At the newly established Jewish High School, we sat in on Hebrew classes. It was heartwarming to find a resurgence of Jewish life in Germany, even if it is slow. With the influx of Jewish immigrants from Russia, the Jewish population in Germany is now up to 80,000. Today, instead of Jewish institutions being burned down while police watch and do nothing, German police protect Jewish sites. In the heart of Berlin a beautiful Jewish museum just opened. The director, Michael Blumenthal, also a former refugee, lived in the Shanghai ghetto during the war. Blumenthal was Secretary of the Treasury under President Carter.

When we visited Bergen-Belsen, the notorious death camp that claimed the life of Anne Frank, we saw pictures of ovens, gas chambers, and stacks of corpses in the adjacent museum. As the students and I conducted a memorial service, a number wept openly, in disbelief. In spite of abundant evidence, there are still some Holocaust-deniers like David Irving, a well-known American professor from Northwestern University who wrote *The Hoax of the 20th Century*. It is true that along with the six million Jews who perished, one third of the Jewish world population, a large number of Poles, Gypsies, homosexuals, and communists were also murdered. The Final Solution, however, was an unprecedented plan aimed exclusively at totally destroying the Jewish people.

Our California group visited synagogues in Bonn, Hamburg and Berlin, where I was invited to sing at some of the services. Hearing again a few of the melodies I remembered from my youth brought tears to my eyes. At the end of the worship services we sang the Israeli National Anthem—*HaTikvah*, The Hope—ending with the words "*Od Lo Avdah Tikvatenu*"—we have not lost our hope.

Elie Wiesel, winner of the Nobel Prize for Literature, said about the Holocaust, "There are many questions and no answers." The concept of *forgiving*—the dominant theme of Yom Kippur—inspired questions for me and for the students as we returned home. Can I really forgive the horrors my people have suffered? I can forgive only the suffering I personally endured. The only ones who can truly forgive are not alive, the victims who died at the hands of the Nazis.

The 18th century Rabbi Nachman of Bratzlav wrote a beautiful song entitled *Kol Ha-olam Kulo*, whose words mean,

> *". . . The whole world is a very narrow bridge,*
> *But the main thing is not to be afraid. . ."*

We went to Germany to build bridges, not walls. And in this spirit, we succeeded beyond our expectations.

# Chapter Thirty-Nine

# Gift of the Sabbath

Every day brings something new to look forward to. But to me nothing compares with anticipating the beauty of the Sabbath, or *Shabbat* in Hebrew.

Observing the Sabbath as a day of rest, I find a sense of peace and tranquility that sustains me—transcending time and elevating me from material pursuits into a spiritual world. For me, Sabbath prayer and study replace the drudgery of labor and stress, and give both body and soul new vitality.

Of all the religious and social institutions attributed to the Jewish faith, none has enriched man's spiritual well being as much as the Sabbath. I believe the Sabbath stands unrivaled as Judaism's greatest contribution to humanity. It also affected Christianity and Islam, but not everyone understood its value.

For instance, the Roman stoic philosopher Seneca, who lived in the first century, ridiculed Jews for "wasting one seventh of their lives" by observing the Sabbath. Of course during Seneca's time, slavery and servitude were popular and it was unheard of to give a day off to a slave, who was considered one's property. But in the Torah, even slaves had time off and in the Middle Ages, servants in Jewish families were better treated than those in non-Jewish homes.

The Sabbath's moral values are based on the Torah. When teaching adults in our temple, I draw heavily on these values as well as on my own faith in God. In the Bible, the Sabbath is linked to the Genesis story of creation and symbolizes both the virtue of work and the holiness of rest. The holy Sabbath is also mentioned as a day of rest in the Book of Exodus, which concludes with the building of the tabernacle, a house of worship in the Sinai wilderness. As holy and important as that task was, it nevertheless had to cease for the duration of the Sabbath.

The writer Achad Ha-am said, "More than Israel has kept the Sabbath, it is the Sabbath that has kept Israel." The Sabbath is the only holiday mentioned in the Ten Commandments, and in the Talmud the Sabbath is called The Crown of the Law. The earliest Sabbath legislation relates to life in Judaism's early history, so it may seem somewhat anachronistic now. But it was revolutionary three thousand years ago and is still relevant in today's stressful times.

In fact, there's an important relationship and a direct connection between Shabbat and the week's six working days. According to Jewish legend, the Sabbath didn't exist when the world was created, and each day of the week was then twenty-eight hours in length. To create the Sabbath as the seventh day, each of the six days had to relinquish four hours of its previous existence. In this way the Sabbath became a twenty-four-hour day. Through the contribution of the six working days, the Sabbath and the rest of the week became integrally related.

Although in recent decades medical science and technology have progressed more than in the prior two thousand years of Western civilization, the levels of ethics and morality have remained relatively unchanged. Nevertheless, the rabbis generally perceive the Bible and science as compatible, citing the Torah's words:

> "... Behold, I have given you statues and ordinances that thou mayest *live*—and not die—*by them.*"

The Shabbat statutes and ordinances imply that the quality of our lives is very much influenced by our daily actions. When love, honest labor, and goodwill prevail during the week, we merit the Sabbath as a day of holiness and rejuvenation. Sabbath observance can give us strength to face each new day. On the other hand, a week filled with hatred and strife will not result in Sabbath peace.

The rabbis of old ascribed both moral and spiritual values to the Sabbath. Many concepts that originated in folklore later became concretized over the centuries. For example, Orthodox Jews interpreted the First Commandment (Be fruitful and multiply) along with the idea of Sabbath pleasure and thus concluded that sexual relations were a *mitzvah* on Shabbat.

As an educator, along with my cantorial duties I have derived much satisfaction and pleasure teaching children and adults how the Torah and the Sabbath can help each of us to personally develop and grow. Over the years I had many talented students, and I am proud to say my educational endeavors have born fruit. My cup runneth over.

Four of my students have become rabbis, and they understand the words of their ancient Talmudic sages, who taught that everything a person needs for guidance is found in the Torah.

> "... Turn it over and over; all is in it. . ."

## Chapter Forty

# Recharging My Battery

The Torah refers to the Sabbatical Year as an ecological period that allows the land to rejuvenate itself every seven years by giving it some rest. This fabulous concept of periodic rest every seven years can and should be applied not only to land, but to people as well. Although sabbaticals are most frequently taken by professors, doctors, rabbis, and teachers, they are not the only ones who get "burned out." I believe all working people should have an opportunity —at least every seven years—to take a break and rejuvenate themselves.

Modern medicine has long known the close connection between a state of tension and the physical and mental exertion that can lead to disease. Such ills cannot be cured by just dispensing tranquilizers and sedatives. People need a diversion, a change of pace, and that is what a sabbatical provides. During my tenure at Temple Beth Jacob I was fortunate to be granted three six-month sabbaticals and each time I chose to go to Israel, where I gained a new perspective through relaxation and study.

Cantors don't automatically get sabbaticals. My colleagues have asked me, some with envy, how I managed to arrange such a privilege. I tell them how the first one came about shortly after the Six Day War, when the president of our congregation, Martin Bergman, approached me.

"Cantor, we know how hard you're working for our Temple, but since Rabbi Teitelbaum is due for a sabbatical, we wondered if there might be any part you could take over in addition to your regular responsibilities. And if so, how much extra remuneration would you expect?"

My answer was short and direct. "I think I'm capable of handling the extra work in the rabbi's absence, and I don't expect one extra penny for assuming some of his duties."

Martin was impressed and surprised by my reply.

"However," I continued, "I would like to request that I be given the same consideration—to also be granted a sabbatical when my time comes."

"Well, the matter has to come before the board," Mr. Bergman said.

At the next board meeting, to my great joy, my request was unanimously approved. I had been with Beth Jacob since 1964 and knew that my turn for sabbatical would come in 1977. In the meantime, because I agreed to take over the rabbi's roles, Beth Jacob didn't need to engage an interim rabbi, which meant the synagogue saved a lot of money. Rabbi Teitelbaum and I discussed certain rabbinical duties and he instructed me in the specifics of, for example, performing weddings and funerals during his absence. While he was off on his sabbatical, I was working night and day, doing his job as well as mine.

Prior to my own sabbatical, I spent the year just preparing. Although I was grateful for the opportunity, I certainly had to work hard for it. Most importantly, I trained some of my choir members to lead Sabbath services and scheduled Torah readers from my Trope (*cantillation*) class to take turns for the weekly reading. The only expense Beth Jacob had during my absence was to hire Jeff Schwarz, one of my outstanding former students, to teach the Bar Mitzvah class. Rhoda Keyson, our choir director, trained the choir to sing regularly at Sabbath Eve services.

Our first sabbatical in 1977 was the spiritual adventure of a lifetime. To rest assured that our children were being cared for while we were away, we hired a Scandinavian couple, who needed to be near Stanford, to stay in our house. In Israel we rented an apartment on Rashba Street in the Rechavia section of Jerusalem, my favorite city. Although Eva and I could have chosen to go anywhere during our six-month breaks, each time Israel was our preference. I wanted a place for refreshment, enrichment, study, research, and education. After being in Israel I knew I would come back to work able to contribute even more.

To perfect our modern Hebrew, Eva and I enrolled in a five-month *ulpan*, an intensive language school, for four hours a day, five mornings a week. The ulpan is a phenomenal institution. My advanced class consisted of twenty-five students, primarily newcomers from Russia, Argentina, Canada, the United States, and even an ardent Zionist student from Japan. No English was permitted, so we were allowed to communicate only in Hebrew.

Every day we sang and I saw how music united us, and how songs were being used in a way similar to how I taught my classes at Beth Jacob. The ulpan curriculum was built around the holidays, so for *Tu B'Shvat* (the New Year of the Trees) we learned music about planting and how the early Jewish pioneers revitalized the land of Israel (then Palestine). In the same way we would study Passover, Chanukah, and other special days on the Jewish calendar.

One unforgettable memory of the first ulpan was Ephraim Katzir's visit to our class. To honor Katzir, President of the State of Israel, the teacher asked me to present a short speech and also to sing, so I brought along my guitar. Providing music was easy, however I was a bit nervous about speaking to the President in Hebrew. (My little speech seemed to go well, despite my apprehension.)

For the first sabbatical Eva was able to schedule hers at the same time. This gave her an opportunity to study foreign language instruction in Israel as well as in Sweden, Switzerland and Germany, which we visited on side trips. In July 1977 we both took two weeks off from the ulpan to participate in the *Zimriyah*, the international choir festival. Our Temple Beth Jacob choir arrived and stood between groups from Iceland and South Africa, singing together in a psalm by Felix Mendelssohn. Joining hundreds of choir singers from all over the world, we gave concerts in Kibbutzim and small communities all over Israel, culminating in a joint concert at the Binyaneh Ha-umah auditorium in Jerusalem.

On successive sabbaticals, Eva and I each attended three-month ulpans. As a result, when I returned to Beth Jacob I could more easily converse with our Hebrew teachers and was also able to better read Torah. In general, the experience made me more educated, more interested, and more interesting.

Each sabbatical was a high point of my life and by the last one in 1995 our daughters were grown and independent. During my Israel ventures, I collected many Hebrew songs and prayer melodies to introduce in my junior congregation. I also took over a thousand color slides that enriched my teaching materials. Our religious school students were intrigued to see images that supplemented units on Jerusalem, the Old City, Masada, Egypt, the Holocaust, and others. My restless seventh-graders were so interested that carpool parents complained they had to wait too long for their children because they lingered in my classroom.

Eva and I often talked about our many memories of Israel. We took *tiyulim* (hikes) to the Old City, signed up for a trip to Egypt with professors from Hebrew University, and attended lectures at the Van Leer Institute. We particularly recalled one talk given by Moshe Dayan, the war hero of the Six Day War, shortly before his death. He told of the encounter with the Vichy forces where he lost one eye. The story is told when he was caught speeding on the road from Tel Aviv to Jerusalem and the policeman questioned him. "Didn't you notice you were going too fast?" Dayan replied, "I have only one eye and I must keep it on the road!" The policeman let him off.

To hear lectures by the famous Torah scholar Nachama Leibowitz, I took a bus outside Jerusalem to the Mevaseret Tziyon absorption center (for newly arrived immigrants). A brilliant lady, she had taught in Berlin at the same Adass Yisroel School I attended as a child.

Eva and I visited Jerusalem's Great Synagogue, which had a famous cantor, Naftaly Hershtik, and a magnificent male choir. Although I was always comfortable in an Orthodox service, Eva was not. She did, however, consent to sit in the women's section of the Great Synagogue. Her complaints about the chattering in the women's section reminded me of the joke about two friends who meet in the beauty shop. Both are sitting under a hairdryer, so it's difficult to hear each other.

"Are you coming to *Shul* on Shabbat?" one woman calls out.

"Yes," the friend shouts back.

"Good," the woman replies. "We can talk during services!"

Eva and I often attended the Conservative synagogue on Agron Street in Jerusalem, where men and women sat together. It's ironic, though, that later when we were in our Conservative synagogue—a perfect compromise—we rarely ever sat together because I was always on the bimah and she was usually singing in the choir. We enjoyed hearing lectures by well-known Conservative rabbis such as Simon Greenberg and Israel Goldstein. Sometimes I was even asked to lead services there. Once around Purim, a spring holiday, I conducted a service, while outside, Jerusalem was in the midst of a rare snowstorm. Coincidentally, the Bleibergs, congregants from Beth Jacob, happened to be in Israel, and they surprised me when they entered the synagogue.

In the Judean hills west of Jerusalem, we visited the Ein Karem Hadassah-Hebrew University Medical Center, a marvelous institution that treats Jews and Arabs alike. Eva, a Hadassah member, and I toured the hospital and admired the beautiful Jerusalem windows donated by Marc Chagall. His twelve stained glass depictions of the twelve tribes of Israel surround the interior walls of the small synagogue. We sat there quietly taking in the beauty of Chagall's masterpiece.

On Fridays in Israel all of our activities changed. The streets are alive with shoppers since the stores close at two o'clock in anticipation of the Sabbath. Men carry bouquets of flowers to beautify their homes. As the sun begins to set, a golden glow blankets the eternal city. Eighteen minutes before sundown, a siren goes off to remind women to light candles. Then there is silence. In Jerusalem the busses stop running. Traffic is reduced to a trickle. Groups of men with their children festively dressed walk to their nearby synagogue.

Before one sabbatical I told an accompanist friend in Palo Alto that I was going to Israel. She urged me to look up her brother, Bruno Wassertheil, then chief correspondent for CBS radio. Bruno, an ardent lover of Scrabble, eventually moved to Palo Alto. We played frequently and our friendship lasted until he recently died of cancer. At his request I conducted the memorial service at his funeral, singing "Jerusalem of Gold" and accompanying myself on the guitar.

Prior to each of our trips to Israel, Eva's mother regularly warned us, "It's not a good time to go now." Well, in Israel there are always incidents and terrorism, but Israelis have learned, unfortunately, to live with such intrusions and interruptions, and so must we.

During the sabbaticals in Israel, I was conscious of the country's unrest due to the precarious political situation, the chasm between the religious and secular society, the lack of mutual respect, and the fact that I, as a Conservative Jew, often didn't know where I belonged. Despite all these issues, I have never experienced such a feeling of inner peace as when I was in Jerusalem. How wonderful it would be if another kind of peace could prevail, bringing Arabs and Jews together to live in harmony.

After each sabbatical I returned to my congregation—especially before the High Holy Days—with renewed vim and vigor, filled with a grateful heart eager to continue my work.

## Chapter Forty-One

# What's in a Name?

I have always been fascinated by names and during my long tenure at Temple Beth Jacob, I've had many opportunities to assist in a "baby naming" or *Brith Milah* and witness the continuity of a family.

It's a pleasure and thrill watching the beaming faces of proud parents as they bring their newborn boy to be circumcised or take their newborn girl to the synagogue and ascend the bimah for an *Aliyah* to the Torah. They recite *Shehecheyanu*, the special blessing of gratitude for being alive to celebrate such a joyous occasion, and then everyone sings *Mazal Tov* for congratulations.

Such moving ceremonies are especially significant and always give me new hope, perhaps because one and a half million Jewish children—who each had a name—were lost in the Holocaust, brutally murdered by the Nazis.

I don't remember my own Brith Milah, of course, but I was told that my mother fainted when she first heard my baritone voice giving forth a loud cry during the ceremony.

Over the years I've seen some of the Bar and Bat Mitzvot children I've taught grow up to become brides and grooms who invited me to sing at their weddings. I've also attended the funerals of my students' parents. Sometimes my relationships with families have been so cordial that a new young mother or father would phone and say, "Cantor, you're part of our family! Can you help us to pick a name for our baby?" Such a request is especially meaningful when the new parent is someone whose Brit Milah I myself had officiated at so many years before.

To take part in giving a child a Hebrew name is a special honor. More than just a stamp of identification, a Hebrew name links the generations together. In recent years, a return to Biblical names has been in vogue—Sarah, Rebecca, Joshua, Adam, David, Solomon and so on. Such names reflect the history of our earliest Jewish ancestors.

Sometimes people become curious about the names of others. Not long ago, for instance, a Temple member inquired about my own.

"Hans," he said, "isn't that a typical German name?"

I surprised the congregant by informing him that Hans is actually a Biblical name. I knew this from the thorough research I did before choosing the pseudonym of Johnny Korn when I was in Australia years earlier.

"Hans is the German form of *John* and John is short for *Johann*," I explained. "And Johann is short for *Yohanan,* which in Hebrew means that 'God is gracious.' "

The congregant was even more surprised when I told him that the name of Yohanan, a military commander, appears for the first time in the Book of Jeremiah. In the Book of Ezra another Yohanan, a priest, is mentioned, and in the Book of Maccabees, Yohanan is the name of one of the sons of Mattathias, the Hasmonean priest.

"But the most famous Yohanan of all," I continued, "was Rabbi Yohanan Ben Zakkai, who lived in Jerusalem during the Roman era and witnessed the destruction of the Second Temple."

From further research, I discovered that in Holland the Dutch version of John is *Jan,* pronounced *Yan.* Supposedly, a Dutch man named *Jan Kees* immigrated before the American Civil War to New England. At first only Northerners began to be called *Yankees,* then after the War, that term was applied to all Americans.

My father's name was Max or *Mosheh* in Hebrew. He came from a family of *Cohanim,* descendants of the ancient priestly class. Hence I am proud of my full Hebrew name—*Yohanan Ben Mosheh Hacohen.*

A Jewish name generally signifies the memory of a deceased person, a place, an object, or an event. I am reminded of an amusing story about naming a child according to the Jewish tradition. The parents, it seems, argued about their baby's future name. The mother wanted to memorialize her father, but her husband wanted to use the name of his deceased father. To settle it, they went to their rabbi.

"What was your father's name?" the rabbi asked the husband.

"Nahum," he replied.

"And what was your father's name?" the rabbi asked the wife.

"Nahum," she replied.

"So what's the problem?" asked the astonished rabbi.

"Well, Rabbi," explained the wife, "my father was a pious and learned man, but my husband's father was a drunkard and a cheat. How can we name our son after such an individual?"

The rabbi's answer was clear.

"Name him Nahum anyway, and let time take its course. If he becomes pious and learned, he will know he is named after his mother's father. If, on the other hand, he turns out to be a drunkard and a cheat, he is surely named after your husband's father."

The Book of Genesis begins with the giving or calling of names.

". . . And the *earth* was unformed and void. And God called the light *day* and the darkness *night*. . ."

In Genesis, Adam gives names for all living creatures.

It is not only the ancients who were concerned about names. In the Book of Ecclesiastes we read:

> ". . . *Every man has three names: one his parents give him, one others call him, and one he acquires for himself*. . ."

In the Talmud the significance of names is also discussed.

> ". . . *There are three crowns—the crown of Torah, the crown of Priesthood and the crown of Royalty, but the crown of a Good Name exceeds them all*. . ."

Even William Shakespeare was concerned about names. Perhaps that's why, in *Romeo and Juliet* he had the feuding families pose the famous question, "What's in a name?"

# SICKNESS AND LOSS

## Chapter Forty-Two

# Unwelcome News

For over thirty years I enjoyed professional success as a cantor, and I often reminisced with gratitude about the many challenges and hurdles I had faced and overcome—in Germany, China, Australia, and finally in America. I enjoyed a fulfilling existence, a good marriage, a satisfying career, wonderful children, and grandchildren. What more could anyone ask for?

Then quite unexpectedly came the biggest challenge of my life. I was in excellent health and had been only slightly troubled by a lesion and swelling on the base of my tongue, which was being treated with betacarotene. I hadn't taken the condition seriously until a biopsy showed that the swelling was actually a malignant tumor. Then my general happiness suddenly ground to a halt. I had cancer? A squamous carcinoma? How could that be? The diagnosis hit me like a bombshell. I was devastated and broke down in tears while Eva tried to console me. It was not only the end of my career, I thought, but possibly the end of my life.

Feeling extremely anxious, Eva and I set out one beautiful spring day to Moffet Hospital in San Francisco to meet Dr. Mark Singer, nationally famous Chief of Head and Neck Surgery at Mount Zion Hospital in San Francisco. I was beset with many questions and urgently searching for a solution. Luckily for me, Dr. Singer was not only a physician but also an extraordinary, caring human being with whom I bonded very soon.

The Head and Neck Oncology Department set up a tumor board to evaluate me and recommend a course of action. Chris, a friendly nurse, greeted me, led me into the examination room and onto an elevated chair that resembled the kind a barber uses. To me, though, it felt more like an electric chair to which I was assigned following a death sentence.

Although apprehensive, I tried to wait patiently. After a long half-hour, the room came to life and one by one surgeons, oncologists, residents, interns, and medical students entered. I was the center of attention as they queued up and each one, wearing a glove, looked into my throat and felt around my tongue. After a while, they found what they were looking for—a growing tumor.

"How long have you had this?" one oncologist asked.

I shrugged my shoulders. "I don't know."

"Were you a smoker?" inquired a surgeon.

"No."

"Were you a drinker?" asked an oncologist.

"No."

When the medical entourage exited, I was left alone once more to await the verdict. Finally Dr. Singer returned with Eva and we sat together.

"Here's the scenario," he said, listing my options. "The choice is up to you. You can select surgery or radiation or chemotherapy. Or you can choose to do nothing."

Do nothing? "If I choose to do nothing . . ." I began. Dr. Singer immediately ruled that out.

"No," he said, "Choosing to do nothing means you might have just one year to live."

Eva and I decided to seek a second opinion, but specialists at the Stanford tumor board came to the same conclusion. I was again devastated.

"What are my best chances?" I asked the surgeons.

"Either we cure you—or we don't," was the curt reply.

Eva and I returned to San Francisco to confer once more with Dr. Singer. He suggested a surgical procedure, one that would probably take seven hours.

"What are my chances?" I asked with trepidation.

"I'm sure you'll make it, Hans," he said compassionately, putting his arm around me. "But I don't know if I will!"

Surgery was scheduled for the following week. Until then time stood still. Nights were sleepless. Days were restless. Little did I know what was in store for me. I had to remind myself that in my long career as a clergyman I had seen many people in pain, suffering from and succumbing to cancer. And they had turned to me for solace. To whom shall I turn now, I asked myself.

"Have a positive attitude, Hans," my friends urged, trying to cheer me up. "Don't worry, you'll be fine. We'll come to visit you," they promised. I tried my best to keep a stiff upper lip, determined to be brave like a soldier going into battle. After all, my preoperative examination showed I was strong and in fine shape.

The waiting finally came to an end and it was time for the surgery. I came through it beautifully but not unscathed. After removing half of my tongue, Dr. Singer reconstructed the remaining part by taking a skin graft from my right thigh, a rectangle of tissue about four by six centimeters. The surgery was followed by seven grueling weeks of radiation, which were especially painful toward the end. By the last week, I was ready to give up.

With faith, hope, and daily prayer, though, I was especially mindful of the prophet Jeremiah's supplication, "Heal me, and I shall be healed." For days I lay silent, unable to speak. With a chalkboard in my hand, I was able to communicate with the doctors and nurses. As each week passed, the tubes were removed one by one. I learned more about my affliction from the many professionals who cared for me, more experts than I had ever seen before. In addition to Dr. Singer, there were oncologists, a radiologist, a plastic surgeon, my primary physician, an endocrinologist, a prothodontist, a dentist, a speech therapist, a nutritionist, a dermatologist, a pharmacist, a dental hygienist, and a number of fine nurses.

Fortunately my larynx was not affected. Although I had to learn to speak all over again, I could still sing. As the mending process began, I became aware of all the medical machinery. An N.G. tube in my nose to feed me. A morphine drip to ease my pain. An I.V. bottle hanging by my bedside. An oxygen tank to help me breathe. A catheter inserted into my urethra.

Finally, I was discharged and Eva drove me home. That night I retired with a kiss, a warm embrace from Eva, and her goodnight words, "I'm glad I've got you, Hans."

Healing took many months. Music—especially Mozart in the morning—lifted my soul and spirits, and the Psalms gave me inspiration.

*Yea, though I walk through the valley*
*of the shadow of death I shall fear no evil,*
*for Thou art with me.*
                    *—Psalm 23*

## Chapter Forty-Three

# It Just Doesn't Fit

A company in Menlo Park goes by the egregious name of "Failures." Such an incongruous name certainly doesn't inspire confidence, yet the company has been successful for many years. In fact, "Failures" actually specializes in reducing stress and analyzing the causes of disaster.

I'm fascinated by the phenomenon of failure and how it can, paradoxically, turn around to be a success. Throughout history many people have confronted unlikely situations and managed to come out ahead. Two distinguished Englishmen who come to mind are Benjamin Disraeli and Winston Churchill.

In 1868 Benjamin Disraeli became Prime Minister of England when Queen Victoria knighted him and conferred on him the title Earl of Beaconsfield. Disraeli had a number of career failures earlier, though. In fact, he wrote, "Failure, when sublime, is not without its purpose." He was heckled and hooted down with catcalls when he pleaded on behalf of the Tories, a political party in England. Despite such incidents, he remained an optimist.

"Though I sit down now," he told his Parliament colleagues, "the time will come when you *will* listen to me."

His words of admonition eventually came true. Disraeli's tenacity paid off and he continued to advance his career in spite of being confronted by anti-Semitism. For Disraeli, failure was simply a challenge to overcome.

Sir Winston Churchill, the greatest statesmen of the last century, also developed a similar attitude toward failure. In the United Kingdom it was common knowledge that he certainly failed to have healthy habits. He rarely had a restful night's sleep, his stress level was very high throughout his life, he was obese, had extremely high cholesterol, and dined on breakfasts featuring champagne and lobster. Churchill was also a smoker, rarely seen without puffing on a big cigar.

With the lifestyle he followed, statistics would have predicted an early demise. Instead, he challenged the statistics and died at the ripe old age of ninety-one. It just doesn't fit! In his political life, Churchill also suffered many setbacks. Yet, as a Conservative in the British Parliament, his career was indeed a success story. During World War II when the chips were down and Londoners were experiencing the Blitzkrieg, his motto was, "We shall never surrender." Churchill exemplifies how one can courageously face drastic situations and still emerge successfully.

In my own case, over the years I've worked hard to maintain good health and found in Judaism elements that support my efforts. The rabbis of the Talmud didn't have the advantages of today's modern science, but their appreciation of the marvelous construction of the human body is reflected in Judaism's daily morning prayers.

Upon awakening one is commanded to wash hands and recite a blessing thanking God for the gift of life and the wonders of our physical makeup. I begin my own daily morning prayers with a blessing of thanks for the magnificent construction of my body, its organs and vessels, and for the privilege to reawaken refreshed and healthy, ready to face the challenges of a new day.

*". . . Praised are You, O Lord our God, King of the universe, who has*
*given us bodies, marvelous in structure, intricate in design, and*
*wonderful in function. Should but one of them, by being broken,*
*fail to function, it would be impossible to exist. . ."*

Nearly a thousand years after the rabbis of the Talmud, another great rabbi wrote a treatise on medicine. Maimonides, who was also a physician, lived in the 12th century but he was far ahead of his time. He advised his patients that the essential ingredients for good health include sunshine, exercise, and fresh air, especially at the seashore.

I have faithfully followed ancient Jewish advice as well as modern updates on how to be healthy. But when I was diagnosed with cancer, the automatic first response was what had I done wrong? Where did I fail?

Then, after a time of reflection, I realized that I didn't fail at all. Yes, I had led a very productive life. Yes, I had allowed time for exercise, following Cicero's dictum, mens sana in corpore sano (a healthy mind in a healthy body). Yes, I was neither a smoker nor a drinker, and good nutrition was always important to me. Religiously I swallowed vitamins A, C, and E as key nutrients to keep my body strong. I kept my weight at an acceptable level due to a careful diet. I practiced yoga and meditation, following the present trend of holistic medicine designed to help one avoid stress.

I was doing all the right things, so it just didn't fit that I should get cancer. I could ponder the question of why I got it, but was there really any answer? The mysteries of life are often out of our hands. There's no explanation other than that I was just another victim of circumstance. I harbor no guilty feelings about the cause of my illness because I played the game the best I knew how. But even correct actions don't always bring about desired solutions. Although I had all the right pieces, they just didn't add up. One has to be lucky, too.

That reminds me of the story about a man in Israel who won a lottery by choosing number 48.

"I don't understand it," the man's perplexed friend said. "How could 48 possibly win when everyone knows the winning number had to be a multiple of seven?"

"Well, I won anyway," replied the man.

"Yes," the friend insisted, "but 49 is a multiple of seven—not 48."

"So?" asked the man.

"So how did you choose 48?" the confused friend asked.

"Aha," answered the man. "That's where mazal (luck) comes in."

I have experienced a lot of mazal in my life, and I've chosen optimism as my steady diet. Like Tevya in Fiddler on the Roof, my cup is also half full rather than half empty. Over a glass of wine Tevya toasts "To Life, to Life, Lechayim." I too love life with all its ups and downs. For the last seventy-nine years, I have come close to the edge many times but by spiritually exploring the recesses of my inner space, hope, and faith have always sustained me.

In The Sound of Music the lyrics of "My Favorite Things" include such charming items as raindrops on roses and whiskers on kittens. For me, failure is not one of my favorite things. I am not one to give up easily. When it comes even to the small things, I'm the kind who always manages, for instance, to get tickets for concerts that are supposed to be sold out. When it comes to being a cancer survivor, I've learned to take one day at a time.

But I agree with Sholem Aleichem, the great Yiddish writer who said: "Never give up—even if it kills you!"

# Chapter Forty-Four

# On Not Giving Up

Religious faith and an optimistic outlook sustained me, and I was determined to carry on but two years later the cancer recurred. This time even more extensive surgery was necessary. A titanium jawbone replaced my own in a procedure that involved a tongue-jaw-neck dissection, reconstruction of the pharynx with a flap of skin from my forearm, removal of the mandible, a tracheotomy, and then plastic surgery.

For weeks I was fed with a naso-gastric tube. Since I was unable to eat solid food, many friends and members of my congregation brought soups and blended meals. That kindness as well as hundreds of cards, gifts, books, and videotapes kept me going. My wife of forty-eight years, God bless her, was by my side day and night to give me support.

In spite of the challenges of adapting to my changed physical condition, I continued my post as cantor at Beth Jacob for the next four years until I retired at the age of seventy-one. Then Eva and I became busy with many activities. Once a week we enjoyed folk dancing and I even volunteered to teach it at Beth Jacob. I also joined four clubs: a Creative Writers Club in order to write my autobiography; a Computer Club to give me the facility to record my words; a Health Club to take care of my body through exercise and swimming; and the Lost Chord Club, a group of larynjectomees who met weekly and shared their experiences.

I realized, of course, that my life would never be the same. Every six months I still see Dr. Singer for regular check ups. He always greets me with, "Here comes my star patient!" Then he introduces me to the entourage of residents who surround him. To be told, "You are cancer free!" is music to my ears. The visit always ends with a hug and "Keep up the good work, Hans!"

Strange as it seems, I have derived some benefits from my illness. For example, I used to dread Novocain at the dentist, but now I rarely need it since my jaw and lips are still numb from radiation. I used to have a beard but because radiation burned off the hair, the skin on my cheeks is so smooth that shaving is barely necessary. Before my operation I used to lecture, present talks on Jewish music and history, and give sermons when the rabbi was away. Because of my speech impediment, talking is tedious, so instead I have turned more to reading and writing. I have also intensified my listening skills by hearing more and talking less, which we all should probably do. After all, God gave us two ears and only one mouth.

Since my illness I have received more attention as well as compliments. Everybody says, "You look wonderful. How do you feel?"

Due to the side effects of radiation-induced dysphasia, which destroyed my salivary glands, I suffer from dry mouth and have difficulty in swallowing so my food still must be blended. As a result, though, I'm forced to eat slowly, which is healthier, and I must work at keeping my weight up at a satisfactory level. Positive attitude!

When the great Albert Schweitzer was in his forties, he became ill and believed his future was uncertain. After undergoing two operations, he recovered fully and wrote *On the Edge of the Primeval Forest*. I often think of Schweitzer's words:

> *". . . The misery I have seen gives me strength and faith in the future.*
> *I do hope I shall find a sufficient number of people who, because*
> *they themselves have been saved from physical suffering, will*
> *respond to those in need. . ."*

I share Schweitzer's sentiment, which helps me continue to ease the suffering of others. Through prayer and the voice of melody that comes from the soul, I am blessed with the ability to touch people who are celebrating happy events as well as those who are bereaved. When I visit Temple members who are ill, it's easier to give encouragement because I speak from my own experience with hardship and suffering. I know firsthand how illness can deprive one of opportunities to fulfill dreams and aspirations.

I often recommend to congregants books I've read that helped teach me the importance of not giving up even when burdened by illness. I've been inspired by sources including Healing Words by Larry Dossey; Love, Medicine and Miracles by Bernie Siegel; Kitchen Table Wisdom, by Rachel Naomi Remen; and above all the perennial bestseller, The Bible.

My favorite TV station is the Wisdom Channel, which I watch while I eat. It deals with holistic medicine and the philosophy of body and mind. I've also been inspired by a story about the great violinist Paganini, who gave a powerful demonstration of not giving up even under a very dismal circumstance. Once in the middle of a concert, a violin string broke. Undaunted, he played on until a second broke. As the stunned audience watched, fate had a third string also break. Paganini didn't stop. Giving it his all, he concluded the concert on one string. Such tenacity of mind and spirit is impressive. I too have learned not to give up. I still keep singing even with the limited resources I possess.

Having a pleasing voice was a wonderful gift given to me by God. But everyone's voice naturally diminishes with age, and mine has too. Vocally I was always able to express my innermost feelings with music, which is the breath of life to me. I once had a two-and-a-half octave range but my voice now has changed from baritone to deep bass. Fortunately, my vocal chords are okay and—most important—I can still sing! Positive attitude!

As I reflect on my illness, I believe that hope is always on the horizon, and I can still play a role and contribute my bit to make the world a better place. As a cancer survivor, every morning I give thanks. Each new day is like a birthday present that I unwrap with a prayer of gratitude, wondering what awaits me in the ensuing hours. The gift of life fills my heart and deepens my awareness of each moment. Knowing that our days on this earth are numbered heightens our realization that time is precious. Love is the essential ingredient that makes life worthwhile. In my lifetime I have received a great measure of love, and my greatest happiness is to share it with others.

I learned early in life that material wealth does not always bring happiness in the long run. In fact, the more we have the greater our appetite for further increasing our possessions. We come into this world empty-handed and we take nothing with us when we leave.

Reminding myself that cancer is a word and not a sentence, I recall the lyrics of a song Johnny Mercer wrote long ago:

> "... You've got to ac-cent-tuate the positive, e-liminate the negative,
> Latch on to the affirmative; don't mess with Mister in-between.
> You've got to spread joy up to the max-imum,
> Bring gloom down to the mini-mum
> Have faith . . . or pandemonium li'ble to walk upon the scene. . ."

## Chapter Forty-Five

# Humor Without Hurt

Even though I vowed to fight and survive both cancer surgery and radiation, I still wondered what else I could do. Meditation, daily prayer, spiritual guidance, and maintaining a positive attitude were all helpful actions; nevertheless, I wanted to discover still another treatment. Searching for an answer, I amassed a library of fine books and in the course of my investigation learned something important—that laughter and a sense of humor can help bring about physical healing.

In *The Anatomy of an Illness,* author Norman Cousins describes how a sense of humor lessened his lingering pain. Creating his own kind of therapy, Cousins sometimes stayed in a hotel and rented funny movies starring comedians like Groucho Marx, Red Skelton, and Bob Hope. He enjoyed them without the interruptions and distractions of home. Through humor he was able to feel better without medication. He wrote,

> "... I made the joyous discovery that ten minutes of genuine
> belly laughter has an anesthetic effect and would give me
> at least two hours of pain-free sleep. . ."

Cousins, who shares my admiration for the great Albert Schweitzer, discovered a surprise about the great doctor when visiting him in Lambarene, French Equatorial Africa. In spite of living under deplorable conditions while caring for lepers at his jungle hospital, this famous Nobel Prize winner incorporated two unusual components into his medical treatment: music and humor. He believed that music had a healing quality and that laughter provides a vital nourishment. Schweitzer told amusing stories or timely jokes as part of his therapy while recovering from serious illness.

In his book *Laughter Incorporated*, Bennett Cerf, author and comedian, claimed his psychiatrist often advised him, "Don't take yourself so damned seriously!" The famous comedian Bob Hope, whom I admire greatly, lived to the ripe old age of one hundred. He said, "I have seen what a laugh can do. It can transform almost unbearable tears into something bearable and hopeful."

While ill, I too discovered that laughter could raise my spirits. While still in the hospital after surgery, I started telling jokes although I was hooked up with wires, intravenous feeding, and tubes through all the orifices of my body. I even got the doctor to chuckle when I invited him for lunch. We had a good laugh together.

Modern research has documented the notion that a sense of humor has therapeutic value. Humor can lower the level of stress hormones and strengthen the immune system. We all need to laugh more! The idea of using humor to alleviate illness made a lot of sense to me because since I was a child I had been telling and collecting jokes and humorous stories.

As a teacher I spiced my classes with amusing tales and anecdotes. Although I was tough and strict with my students, humor was part of my teaching strategy. I have a file folder filled with comical stories so whenever I made a presentation I always introduced it with a personal experience or joke. To this day when I hear a good anecdote or amusing story, I write it down.

One of my many "doctor" jokes is about a patient who can't afford surgery, so the doctor touches up his x-ray. Or maybe you heard about a man who has a sore foot? The doctor tells the man, "I'll have you walking in an hour." He did. The doctor stole his patient's car.

Perhaps one of the earliest mentions of humor appears in the Book of Genesis. When God tells Sarah, the aged wife of Abraham, that she will bear a son, she laughs. But when Isaac arrived, the parents named him in Hebrew— *Yitzhak*—which means "he will laugh."

The importance of humor in life was also recognized in the Biblical Book of Ecclesiastes, whose timeless words are still relevant to us today. Through humor he was able to feel better without medication. He wrote,

*"For everything there is a season and a time for every purpose under the heavens. . . A time to weep and a time to laugh. . ."*

The Jewish people have been persecuted throughout history and discriminated against up to this day, but they can't continuously weep. Probably as an antidote, Jews developed a sense of humor, and perhaps that's why a disproportionate number of comedians are Jewish. They joke a great deal even through adversity. Our survival is a miracle so we have much reason to rejoice and also to laugh.

Even in the Nazi concentration camps, many humorous stories were told, helping ease pain by keeping up an indomitable spirit of hope. While languishing in Auschwitz and other horrible death camps, Jews made jokes to find relief. One story was told about Hitler, who consults a psychic because he is curious about his future.

"You're going to die on a Jewish holiday," the psychic predicts.

"On which holiday?" Hitler inquires.

"It doesn't matter," replies the psychic. "Any day you die will be a Jewish holiday!"

Through the ages, humor has been comforting. In *Laughter Incorporated*, Bennett Cerf quotes the advice of a Jewish philosopher: "When you laugh, you give yourself the courage not to grieve." In *Treasury of Jewish Humor*, Nathan Ausubel tells a story through dialog.

"How are things?"

"Good."

"Good? You seem to have plenty of troubles."

"No. It's always good! In the summer I'm good and hot, in the winter I'm good and cold. My roof leaks, so when it rains, I'm good and wet. Furthermore, my nagging wife makes me good and mad. Believe me, I'm good and tired of it all!"

When I visit patients in the hospital I often run into the Monsignor of the San Mateo Diocese. One of the stories we frequently trade concerns a sinking boat.

"Does anyone here know how to pray?" asks the captain.

"I do," answers a man confidently.

"Good," the captain replies. "You pray and the rest of us will put on life jackets. We're one short."

A good sense of humor is universal, relieves worry and tension, and has no ethnic limitations. We all need to laugh more and worry less. Wilfred Peterson, a writer, says it beautifully: "He who laughs — lasts."

The words of an old song come to my mind:

> ". . . *When you're smiling, the whole world smiles with you,*
> *When you're crying, you cry alone.* . ."

# Chapter Forty-Six

# Food for Thought

My passion for food began while I was a teenager in Shanghai. Malnutrition and starvation were common occurrences then, so very few people could enjoy the pleasures of eating. During those harsh war years, I learned that only the individual who personally experiences hunger can really understand it. My choice to become a cook not only alleviated such hardship; it helped my father and me to survive.

Eating is more, though, than just the process of bringing fuel to one's body. The social aspects of food are also an integral component of nourishment. Although I was a child when we lived in Berlin, I still vividly remember the times my parents and I sat together at the table, sharing ideas as well as food. Because of our fear of Nazis we had to be careful with words, so the windows were shut and the curtains drawn. I recall how my father's hushed voice commingled with the aroma of the tasty meal my mother prepared. The smell of the chicken soup—without the fat skimmed off—sparked my appetite; in those days the risks of high cholesterol were unknown.

Since my early years I was intrigued by the history of food and fascinated by the literature of gastronomy. For centuries food has been linked with the ethnic lifestyles of humans, beginning with the first inhabitants on earth, who ate fruits and vegetables to sustain themselves.

The Bible, beginning with the Book of Genesis, provides examples of the significance of food. Abel, a farmer, shared his food by offering sacrifices to the deity. Jacob, who must have been a fine cook, prepared lentil soup to get his brother Esau's birthright. Their mother, Rebecca, helped Jacob concoct a venison delicacy in order to receive his father's blessing. After Noah lived forty days in the ark to escape the flood, he planted a vineyard and got stone drunk to celebrate being back on dry land. When three angels visited

Abraham in his tent, he hospitably welcomed their company and instructed Sarah to cook a calf with cream sauce.

The word *company* comes from the Latin *com*, which means *together* and *panis* or bread; hence, *company* literally means to break bread together. "Bread, the staff of life" is frequently mentioned in Scripture. Today matzah, the traditional unleavened bread, is still eaten during the Passover Seder to celebrate the ancient Israelites' exodus from Egypt. In Christian Scripture the most famous dinner is of course The Last Supper, the Passover Seder at which Jesus broke bread, drank wine, and shared with his disciples. Rituals and customs regarding the use and preparation of food can be found in the *Leviticus*, the Biblical book replete with dietary regulations known as *Kashrut*.

A very old axiom is "Nurture shapes Nature" or as the Germans used to say, *Der Mensch ist was er isst*. Over the centuries, a whole gastronomical literature developed along with many myths, giving food consumption a deeper meaning. Each group of people maintains their own ethnicity, creating distinctive cuisine and food specialties. Among my favorite foods are French and Chinese.

In my youth I loved to eat and devoured huge meals. What I missed out during the hungry periods in Shanghai I later amply made up for in my sojourn first to Australia and then in America. My favorites included roast beef and potato dumplings as well as whipped cream and strawberries, something I rarely had in China because they were so expensive. After I sold my restaurant in Carmel, California and became a cantor, food and cooking was no longer a career, it became a hobby.

Both my life and my relationship with food, however, drastically altered in 1994 after my cancer surgery. The pleasure of eating was gone and my fine palate underwent many stages of adjustment. Before, I looked forward to eating; now I'm always happy when I'm finished because the process is not only wearisome but also time consuming. In addition, when food is pureed and whipped together, you never get the real flavor.

Now I eat in order to live, but sometimes I do think longingly about the old days. One restless night while I was recuperating, I ate a bagel with lox and cream cheese plus coleslaw on the side. It seemed to taste especially good since I hadn't anything like that for so long. I was delighted, too, because I had no problem getting it down.

"My swallowing has been solved," I rushed to tell Eva. "From now on, no more blending!"

Then the alarm clock rang, waking me to get ready for my morning exercise class. Wishful thinking! It was all only a dream, so I went to the kitchen to prepare my breakfast, cream of wheat or oatmeal blended with a scrambled egg, some honey and almond butter. My taste buds are not what they used to be, but I have also developed a special nutritious breakfast drink—apricot juice, banana, and prunes all blended together with vitamin supplements. Since I'm on liquid food I have no weight problem. My only concern is to maintain it. I still enjoy cooking, though, and when my children visit I prepare tasty dinners for them and puree my own. They especially love my homemade soups and my tuna and salmon casseroles.

Cooking, I believe, has a tremendous therapeutic value. Not many people realize it's the only creative activity that calls on each of our five senses. We carefully *touch* and prepare the ingredients with our hands. I take liberty to create dishes that have appeal to the *eye*. The *smell* of the food stimulates our appetite, and we choose proper seasonings that *taste* good to the palate. Last but not least, my creations evoke complimentary speech—*words* of praise. Often I invite guests, serve them a nice meal and love to see them enjoying it.

Although I have had both a professional and personal culinary passion, now that my eating is so restricted, I cheerfully realize there's much more to live for besides food. Walking in my garden, smelling the flowers, and beholding the beauty of nature gives me pleasure. I also enjoy regularly participating at the synagogue as well as listening to a Beethoven symphony or enjoying many other delights. Music became my soul food.

For inspiration, I say my prayers or grab a good book. Every day I count my blessings, especially when I visit people in the hospital. I know now what it feels like to suffer. Every day is a new day. I am aware that things will never be the same, so I take one day at a time and try to maintain a positive outlook on life.

In this spirit I concur with the Biblical wisdom that says, *"Man does not live by bread alone."*

## Chapter Forty-Seven

# Gestures of Love

In February 2000 Eva and I celebrated our fiftieth wedding anniversary with a dinner dance at the Stanford Park Hotel. Becki, Ruth, and Barbara—our three daughters—came with their spouses and children along with many close friends who joined us for an evening of music and poetry. As many well-wishers showered us with admiration and expressions of affection and love, Eva and I sat together, holding hands, listening to accolades and a replay of years of joys and sorrows.

Ours was indeed a match made in heaven. How fortunate we were to have enjoyed a perfect union for five decades and how thankful for so many blessings. We didn't have a fancy, handwritten, artistic *ketuba* (traditional Jewish marriage certificate) as is so popular today, but our love for each other was engraved upon our hearts. We were one in body and spirit. We never imagined this anniversary celebration would be the last happy event our whole family would share.

When my agent contacted me about serving as chaplain during Passover on a Mediterranean cruise, Eva and I were overjoyed. After accepting the Royal Caribbean Line's invitation, we immediately purchased our airline tickets to Dubai via London. I prepared my religious services and music, and as the departure date approached we were getting ready to pack our bags for the trip. But then something unexpected and disturbing began happening.

"I don't feel quite right," Eva said several times.

She had noticed some problems with her right hand, and I too was aware that she was constantly dropping things. While playing the piano, she was uncharacteristically striking wrong notes, and while writing at her computer, a surprising number of typos began to appear. Eva's condition concerned me.

"Eva, you'd better call the doctor," I urged.

On a Tuesday, less than two weeks before our scheduled cruise, Eva described her symptoms to her primary care physician, Dr. Cheryl Gold, who asked her to come the following day to the Palo Alto Clinic. Little did we know what awaited us. Suspecting either a stroke or a brain tumor, the doctor had Eva go through a battery of high-tech tests, including an MRI of the brain and a CAT Scan. Within twenty-four hours we learned the shocking diagnosis: a brain tumor.

On Thursday, worried and nervous, we met with the neurosurgeon, who examined Eva, ordered more tests, and told us he thought the tumor could be removed. As part of routine pre-op procedures, Eva was instructed to get a chest X-ray and expect to be admitted to Stanford for surgery the following Monday. We were both in a state of shock and of course I canceled our trip, just ten days before the departure date.

On Friday we sat in the patio having lunch. It was a warm and beautiful day, and each of us was lost in thoughts of concern and uncertainty, but we were still optimistic that Eva's upcoming surgery would solve her problem. Then the phone rang. It was the neurosurgeon.

"I have some unexpected news," he said quietly. "The X-ray showed a mass in the right lung, but nevertheless we'll go ahead with the surgery."

A mass in the right lung? Another bombshell!

Feeling numb and devastated by this new problem, both Eva and I broke down and cried. Confused, she called Dr. Gold for guidance. Although it was Saturday, the doctor conferred with a number of expert physicians to decide on a course of action.

"Let's cancel the brain surgery," Dr. Gold advised. "The mass on the lung must be treated first so we should spare Eva from going through the agony of an operation." Then more bad news continued coming. After the oncological radiologist examined Eva's lung biopsy, we learned that the tumor was malignant and inoperable.

More tears. We had important decisions to make and needed to quickly set things in motion. We agreed to try chemotherapy and chose Dr. Paula Kushlan, a competent oncologist who was also both a caring physician and a friend.

"We can treat this, so let's be hopeful," the radiologist consoled us.

Despite a very heavy heart, I continued attending my creative writing class, perhaps as an escape from reality. The cat was already out of the bag since everyone knew about Eva's health crisis. In my whole lifetime of attending classes, I have never been showered with so much love and emotional closeness as I was during this terrible time. Barbara Noble, our teacher, was a shining example of a compassionate person.

None of my classmates had ever met Eva, but they acted as though she were a family member. One person came to our house and brought delicious food. Other classmates and Temple members sent flowers, cards, messages of healing, and wrote letters so heartwarming they moved us to tears. Their kindness lit up the darkness that beset us and their concern and affection helped Eva and me to believe that the chemotherapy would restore her to good health. Words fail to adequately express my gratitude.

In the words of Lao-tze (Sixth century B.C.), *"A constant giver is the man who loves."*

## Chapter Forty-Eight

# She Taught Me How to Die

More tears. More tests.

After a CT scan the doctor determined that the mass on Eva's lung was the primary tumor, and it had metastasized to the brain. A microscopic examination showed a small "oat cell," supposedly a curable type of cancer.

A glimmer of hope.

More tests. A biopsy, echocardiogram, tissue exams by a pathologist, X-rays, MRIs, a diagnostic sigmoidoscopy, and surgical removal of the lymph nodes. Already Eva's hair began to fall out from the chemotherapy, so we purchased a beautiful wig made out of human hair, wavy with a salt and pepper texture.

"The wig looks better than my real hair," Eva smiled sheepishly. But she was quite positive and declared, "I know my own hair will grow back."

Being a nature lover, Eva adored flowers so I hoped that a lovely garden would give her pleasure and help her to recover or at least extend her life. We engaged a landscape artist who redesigned our front lawn and our backyard. The new plans included completely resurfacing the patio, uprooting all the dead trees, and removing old bushes, weeds, and dandelions. An array of ferns and flowers—iceberg roses, lilies, camellias, fuchsias, and jasmine—formed a glorious carpet bursting with the colors of the rainbow. We also added trees—lemon, Japanese maple, and moonglow. A new Sukkah, to celebrate our harvest festival, replaced the old one. To make watering easy, we installed a new, computerized irrigation system.

"Too bad we can't go on the Passover cruise," Eva sighed with regret. "But we'll certainly enjoy the summer sitting in our new patio," she said, trying to cheer me up.

Eva's decline happened fast, and our only glimmer of hope faded when Dr. Kushlan announced that the cancer was incurable. We wondered what could have caused the lung tumor. Eva didn't smoke. She was a teacher, so she needed annual chest X-rays, which were always normal. Just before Passover, Eva, weakened by drugs and chemotherapy, had to be hospitalized. She had difficulty breathing as fluid started to build up around her heart sac, but a surgical procedure drained the fluid and gave her some relief. Eva's strength was declining quickly.

I was going around in circles, spending days at the hospital and cooking Eva's favorite foods at night. She had no appetite, but my chicken noodle soup seemed to agree with her. On Passover eve I canceled the holiday evening with the children and instead came to the hospital to spend the Seder night with Eva. In a suitcase, I carried all the necessary items including a Seder plate, a Hagaddah (the Passover narrative), and matzo ball soup. At her hospital bedside we prayed, sang, and ate.

Eva loved life and even in her weakened condition, her convivial smile was infectious. "Together we'll beat this. I know it isn't the end," she insisted. "We have good doctors to help us, so we must be optimistic."

With a heavy heart, I composed myself and replied, "I'm with you all the way."

After about forty-five minutes she began to tire and dozed off. I packed up the suitcase and came home exhausted. I was still hoping against all odds that maybe, somehow, she would be cured and we could resume our wonderful life together.

Eva stayed in the hospital for a week and was released on the Monday after Passover. A friend and I picked her up—bringing along a new wheelchair armed with a portable tank of oxygen to alleviate her breathing difficulties. At home we ordered a regular oxygen tank to be delivered.

Now our last and only hope lay in outpatient chemotherapy treatments at the Palo Alto clinic. Although obviously feeling miserable, Eva never complained.

"My mother lived to be ninety-one," she confidently reminded me.

Although the chemotherapy was going well, fluid around her heart began to build up again, and her illness took a turn for the worse. She began going downhill again, faster this time.

But Eva was still optimistic. "We'll beat this," she declared again.

I knew better, but didn't want to deprive her of hope.

My daughters came to the house and, in despair, I sat with them in the living room. Silence. I sobbed, knowing Eva's days were numbered, but I didn't want her to hear me. When I returned to the bedroom to give Eva her medication, she raised herself up and swallowed the pills.

"Can I get you anything else?" I asked.

"No, thanks," she uttered again, smiling. "I am just so tired, let me rest a little."

Night came. As usual I climbed into bed with her, but sleep was hard to come by. I got up intermittently to take her to the bathroom or give her some water. My mind wandered, pondering the future. I could not envision life without her.

A home health nurse came regularly to wash and help medicate Eva. Our dedicated doctor came to the house too. With sad resignation, Eva and I listened as Dr. Kushlan told us there wasn't much to be done. She did, however, convey the few options that remained.

"We could operate, but you may not survive the surgery," she explained. "If you return to the hospital, you could live a few more weeks. Or," she paused, "you can remain at home, and we would make you comfortable."

Eva made her decision. "I want to remain at home!"

That night I administered some morphine so Eva felt no pain.

On Thursday our children and grandchildren came to say goodbye. Each one approached Eva's bedside to wish her well.

"What's happening?" Eva was astonished. "Am I already checking out?"

Friday, the next day, she took no food and just a little water. As the hours passed, her breathing became more erratic. Haltingly, with abated breath she whispered to me, "I think I'm ready to go. I love you so much."

The day progressed slowly. When the time came to kindle the Sabbath candles, I lit them in the kitchen with our daughters. Mournful and teary-eyed, we did not bring them to Eva in the bedroom because of the danger mixing candle flames with oxygen.

Eva made her last request in an almost inaudible voice. "Please," she said, struggling with every breath, "Sing me my favorite psalm, Essa Enai."

I picked up my guitar and began singing Psalm 121, with the girls harmonizing the melody.

> *". . . Essa enai el he-harim.*
> *I lift up mine eyes*
> *Unto the mountains,*
> *From whence cometh my help. . ."*

Although it was difficult for us, we continued singing for another twenty minutes. As the sun began to set, we closed the curtains and the room grew dim. Soon the Sabbath was upon us. I held Eva. It was almost over. A few difficult breaths, some heaving, then her eyes opened wide for the last time. The end came and I gently closed her eyelids.

I rose. My daughters and I held each other in sorrowful embrace. We were not prepared. It had all come so fast. Although in pain, Eva was courageous throughout her whole ordeal, which took less than two months. She was my soulmate for fifty years and a consummate teacher. On Erev Shabbat she taught me my final lesson—how to die with dignity.

Thinking of Eva, I recall words of love poems from Song of Songs, my favorite book of the Bible.

> "... *For love is strong as death*
> *Harsh as the grave*
> *Its tongues of flames*
> *A fierce and holy blaze*..."

The beautiful flower garden, which we prayed would help her recuperate, we decided to call "Eva's Memorial Garden."

## Chapter Forty-Nine

# Life After Eva

Almost five years have gone by since Eva's death. For fifty years she was the center of my life. Bereaved, I am now on my own and in rebuilding my life I find new strength in reading the Bible.

Happy memories mingle with feelings of loneliness, especially each year as the festival of Passover approaches, reminding me of the last springtime that Eva and I shared. At this season it is traditional in the synagogue to read the Song of Songs, also called Canticles. This group of poems, attributed to King Solomon, symbolizes love and the beauty of nature. I sit in the garden and meditate.

> "... My beloved spoke and said unto me:
> Rise up, my love, my fair one and come away.
> For lo, the winter is past,
> The rain is over and gone;
> The flowers appear on the earth..."

Although I am a people person, there are times I crave solitude and have the urge to distance myself from the mundane, looking for some relief away from the workaday stress. I enjoy the many activities at my Temple and love to interact socially and shmooze with fellow congregants, but it is only when I am alone that I open up to thoughts within me and more deeply breathe in inspiring, life-giving oxygen.

I ask myself, "How can I escape the tension and grief that now envelop me?" Then a still small voice answers, overcoming me with a feeling of spirituality and summoning me to seek solace by venturing forth. Our world is filled with places of tranquility and indescribable beauty, and sometimes the most attractive sites are right near our doorstep if only we look for them.

Ralph Waldo Emerson advised,

> *". . . Place yourself in the middle of the stream of power and wisdom,*
> *Which animates all whom it floats, and you are without effort*
> *Impelled to truth, to right, and perfect contentment. . ."*

Mornings are often beautiful in Palo Alto, where I live. The temperature is mild and when the sun is in full glory, it's a wonderful opportunity for a bicycle ride. Leaving the house, I make my way through city streets toward Highway 101, where an underpass crosses the freeway toward the Bay lands. As I pedal through the noisy tunnel to Shoreline Park, the sound of trucks and cars overhead is deafening.

But once on the other side of the tunnel, the bustle of traffic is behind me and I'm transported into a new world of open spaces interspersed with trails and walkways surrounded by water. As I ride around the curving trails, a peaceful, multicolored landscape unfolds. The clouds overhead are reflected in the calm surface of the water. Lights and shadows stretch out as the morning haze lifts, and the mountains across the lake become visible.

Invigorated by the fresh breeze from San Francisco Bay and in a tranquil mood, I push up the hill toward the reserve where many varieties of birds also come to find refuge with their own species. Majestic pelicans predominate, fishing for their breakfast. An egret with a long white neck stands erect by the shore, appearing one-dimensional, as though waiting in solitude for an unexpected guest. Ignoring the lone creature, sandpipers pass by. A cacophony of bird songs fills the fresh morning air. Overhead a gray hawk, resembling an eagle, searches for food with widespread wings, probably looking for a frog to devour. I encounter a garter snake, undaunted and oblivious of my presence.

In the distance a rabbit speeds along, disappearing in the bushes to escape an enemy. On my right I pass a pair of Canadian geese out for a morning stroll, satisfying their hunger by occasionally nibbling on grass. A group of coots waddle clumsily toward the nearby lake to take a beauty bath. I behold with amazement the beauty of nature at its best. All these creatures seem to live harmoniously side by side. Perhaps there is something we humans can learn from them.

Riding on, I see a group of bird watchers with binoculars make their way up the trail. I overhear one person reporting on spotting an eagle. I don't know what they are looking for, but my goal is to visit some friends who cannot always be spotted. After another mile I finally reach my destination. I'm in luck.

In the distance across a small waterway sit the two burrowing owls I came to visit. Their large broad heads and big eyes stare at me as I park my bicycle by the trail and stand motionless by the roadside, afraid of scaring them if I move closer. We look at each other across the waterway. What, I wonder, is going on in their heads?

"You birds are lucky. How I envy you—having a partner," I murmur. I feel like running away, yearning for Eva, and my own mate. But I am dreaming. I must really face reality.

Sharing the sunlight, the owls and I continue to gaze at each other. Who will make the first move? Caressed by a balmy breeze from the mountains, I look at my watch. It is noon and I must turn back. Overcome with nostalgia I move on, remembering that the lush green carpet formed by the winter rains will soon change to brown with the coming of the dry summer.

"Goodbye, my friends," I call to the owls.

*". . . Life demands from you the strength you possess.*
*Only one feat is possible—not to have to run away. . ."*
—*Dag Hammarskjold*

# LOOKING BACK

## Chapter Fifty

# The Legacy

I did not have a wonderful family life growing up during the Nazi era or in Shanghai. Perhaps that is the reason why I always longed to one day start my own family. For me the Genesis injunction to "be fruitful and multiply" took on new meaning after six million Jewish souls were lost in the Holocaust, among them one and a half million children. Although children are what make a marriage holy and complete, raising children anew became more than a mitzvah; it was essential for the survival and perpetuation of the Jewish people.

I'm grateful that my dream has come true. Eva and I were blessed with three daughters and six grandchildren whom I have watched grow up. The happiest day in our early marriage occurred on September 9, 1952 in Carmel, California when Esther Rebecca arrived on California Admission Day. Eva's mother presented us with three months of diaper service as a baby gift. I quickly learned to change those diapers, often going to work tired from lack of sleep. Becki, as we call her now, cried a lot as a baby and grew up to be an alto.

In 1955, more happiness arrived with the birth of our second daughter, Ruth, on August 6. By then we were experienced parents, and Eva took a leave of absence from teaching to devote herself completely to raising our family.

We were in for a surprise when Eva became pregnant again in 1957. In that year we moved to New York, where I began cantorial studies at Hebrew Union College. Judging from the size of Eva's tummy, we felt so sure it would be a boy we even picked out the Biblical name of David, Israel's king and singer of psalms. But we weren't disappointed when Barbara, our third daughter, was born on January 4, 1958. As she was ready to arrive, I had to borrow a friend's old Chevrolet and drive through a New York snowstorm to get Eva to Flower Hospital on Fifth Avenue.

Coincidentally, Dr. Steinberg was the same physician who had delivered Eva thirty-five years earlier in Dortmund, Germany. Nonchalantly, Eva asked the doctor about the epidural he would administer for the delivery, mentioning that she had read in *Reader's Digest* about this procedure's possible adverse effects.

"I don't get my medical information from the *Reader's Digest*," was Dr. Steinberg's curt reply. The delivery went perfectly.

In my first year at HUC, I remember taking then six-year-old Becki with me on the New York Central train to Croton-on-Hudson, where I taught religious school on Sundays. There she received her first Jewish education, which helped to lay a foundation for her later life.

Ruth began public school in New York while I was a student cantor at the Temple of the Covenant in Uptown Manhattan. Following my ordination, we moved to South Bend, Indiana for my first pulpit and remained there for two years while our girls attended public school. Then our family returned to California and settled in Palo Alto.

After Becki graduated from high school, she spent six months working on a Kibbutz in Israel harvesting fruit, inoculating chickens, and working in the children's house. Later, after graduating from Sonoma State University, she volunteered for a year in Guatemala, helping rebuild the country after its earthquake. She worked as a hospital administrator, an ambulance driver, and even delivered babies.

During a four-year extended stay in Nicaragua, she assisted with the National Literacy Crusade, setting up preschool education, and producing an educational television program. In Managua she met a cameraman, Rito Vargas, who became her future husband.

Returning to the United States with Rito, Becki worked as a teacher like her mother. After earning her Master's degree in education at Hayward State University, she became principal of an Oakland inner city school. Fluent in Spanish, Becki is presently Director of Elementary Education for the Palo Alto School District. She and Rito have three children — Priscilla, Melania, and David. Two presently attend college.

Our daughter Ruth believed, like her sisters, that one should work for an education, so after finishing high school she did housecleaning and also waitressing in San Francisco restaurants. Always an excellent student, Ruth was self-motivated and independent. She too became fluent in Spanish after spending one year in Chile.

She earned her B.A. at the University of California, Santa Cruz, and received her Master's degree in psychology from Antioch University. After completing three thousand hours of social work, she became a licensed psychotherapist and has a thriving practice in Oakland, California. Ruth is in the third level of a three-year training program in sensory-motor psychology, focusing on understanding the nervous system. She is writing a book called *Coming Home to Passion*, which deals with her groundbreaking methods of helping restore loving sexuality for couples who have a history of trauma and neglect.

In a recent letter to me, Ruth said she has a wonderful, satisfying life and she credits my influence for the greatest gifts of her character—relentless determination, endurance, and an ability to work hard, tirelessly and with conviction.

"Those are priceless blessings you taught me both through work and by example," she wrote. "I'm blessed with phenomenal strength which I also feel I inherited from you." Her words of appreciation really touch my heart. Ruth and her husband, Michael Lewin, have two cats and two dogs.

Our daughter Barbara followed in the footsteps of Eva's Aunt Gertrud, who lived in New York and often babysat for us while I studied at HUC. Before coming to America, Gertrud was Director of Nursing at the Jewish Hospital in Hamburg, Germany. Little Barbara admired her great aunt and liked dressing up as a nurse with a cap and medical paraphernalia, giving medicine, and administering shots to her many dolls.

As a school-aged child, Barbara accompanied me to various hospitals on Saturday afternoons and sat in the waiting room while I visited bedridden congregants. It was then that she definitely decided to pursue a career in nursing. Later, in high school, she volunteered as a candy striper at Stanford Hospital and, like her sisters, also did housekeeping and waited tables at a senior retirement community. After completing her public school education in Palo Alto, she earned a B.A. in Nursing from Columbia University and a Master's in Nursing Administration from the University of California in San Francisco.

Barbara now works as a Certified Diabetes Educator at Mount Diablo Medical Center in Concord, California. She is married to Michael Liepman, whose father was my classmate in Shanghai. They live in Richmond, California with their three children, two dogs, and three cats. Benjamin, the oldest, and Julia are in college while Allison just started high school.

Eva and I loved our children deeply and were extremely proud when all chose to enter service occupations, with each daughter finding a niche in her own field. Their careers reflected Eva's lifelong ambitions to be socially involved and to make contributions for the betterment of society.

To this day, I find it difficult to comprehend the loss of my soul mate, Eva. Her passing was a tear in my life's fabric. However, I feel comforted because she left me a precious legacy, three lovely daughters. Through the years she had the joy of having our girls live nearby and seeing six grandchildren grow up.

I continue to feel Eva's presence, though not physical, but I am richly endowed with the genetic treasure she left me. Love never dies; neither does a relationship. There is no time limit on grieving, but the memories and the spiritual strength I have accumulated during the last fifty years with Eva have inspired me to continue on.

I believe death is not the end of our existence on earth because our souls are immortal. Henry Wadsworth Longfellow expresses this sentiment so well in a few verses of my favorite poem, "The Psalm of Life."

> ". . . *Tell me not in mournful numbers,*
> *Life is not an empty dream,*
> *For the soul is dead that slumbers*
> *And things are not what they seem.*
>
> *Life is real! Life is earnest!*
> *And the grave is not its goal;*
> *Dust thou art, to dust returnest,*
> *Was not spoken of the soul. . ."*

# Chapter Fifty-One

# Rain, Rain, Go Away

*". . . Don't know why there's no sun up in the sky, Stormy Weather.
Just can't get my poor self together, I'm weary all the time. . ."*
                                                    —*Porgy and Bess*

It's often said that bad weather can affect the emotions, cause depression, and influence the hormonal system. This is especially true when rain continues for long periods. Even more depressing and upsetting is watching the TV news from our living room and witnessing unfortunate people who have been flooded, lost their homes, and need to be evacuated. Strangely enough the movie feature I chose this rainy evening is an oldie—"Stormy Weather."

On Tuesdays, my regular day for fun and relaxation, I usually try to spend the morning going for a bicycle ride with my friend Jules Zulman, enjoying the open spaces of Shoreline Park, close to my home. But when rain is pouring down, as is often the case in autumn, it's a perfect opportunity to stay indoors. So I retreat to my study, attend to some unfinished business, or perhaps start a new chapter in my book. Then the phone rings.

It's bad news. Jimmy, an old friend, age ninety, is taken to the hospital with a massive stroke. I drop what I'm doing, put on my raincoat, and drive to Stanford Hospital to visit the old man. I try to console his family, but the situation looks hopeless. I say a sad good bye to Jimmy and the next day he slips into eternity. His death is fast and painless. I think of a song—*"Into each life some rain must fall."*

The rain and the news about Jimmy, although expected, affect my mood as I leave the hospital. Back at home, I retreat to the piano and lift my spirits by going over some favorite pop songs. For me, music can do a lot more than just words and speeches. I like all kinds of music, popular and classical. As I

sit down and sing some tunes, it works. I feel better. After all, life has its ups
and downs.

> ". . . *I'm singin' in the rain, just singin' in the rain.*
> *What a glorious feeling! I'm happy again. . ."*

Intermittently I gaze out the window at our front lawn. Heavy rain continues falling. A green carpet of grass has grown up overnight. Maybe it's good
that man cannot control everything. We are still subject to the whims of the
elements, and even though we can predict what the weather will be, forecasts
do little to evoke a change in the course of nature.

I keep turning pages in my songbook and another tune speaks to my mood.

> ". . . *Just let a smile be your umbrella*
> *On a rainy, rainy day. . ."*

I realize we badly need the rain. Without it there would be no life on earth.
Many cultures have prayers and dances for the rain they need to sustain themselves. I think of continents threatened by droughts and the countless people
who have died from hunger. Sitting comfortably in my protected, dry home,
I consider myself blessed. I ponder why there is such an imbalance between
droughts and floods. Then I remember words from Bob Dylan's well-known
song:

> ". . . *The answer, my friend, is blowing in the wind. . ."*

One of my self-help books states that in winter the lack of natural, unfil-
tered sunlight often may lead to melancholy and depression, a condition
called SAD or Seasonal Attitude Disorder. Well, tomorrow is another day and
time passes quickly, so I go off to bed to dream happy dreams.

At seven in the morning, the alarm rings. I jump out of bed to peer through
the curtains. Surprise!

> ". . . *Blue skies, smiling at me.*
> *Nothing but blue skies do I see. . ."*

Trying my luck once again, I get on my bicycle and head for the Bay lands.
What do you know! A dark cloud appears in the distance. A few raindrops begin falling again. Was the sunshine an illusion? Daffodils have made their appearance prematurely due to the abundant rain. I think of another favorite
song made famous by Al Jolson—"April Showers."

> *". . . And when you see clouds upon the hills,*
> *You soon will see crowds of daffodils. . ."*

Riding on, I hear pitter-patter sounds on my bicycle helmet. Sunshine mingling with light rain once again greets me. To be safe, I have my rain jacket with me. Furiously I pedal on to capture the fresh morning air. On the horizon a majestic rainbow stretches out. Getting off my bike, I gaze upon it in wonderment. The first rainbow, the Book of Genesis tells, came when God made a covenant with Noah that there would not be another flood. As I behold the band of color in the sky, a sign of faith and hope, I begin to cheer up from yesterday's depressed state.

I remember Judy Garland in "The Wizard of Oz" singing,

> *". . . Somewhere over the rainbow, skies are blue,*
> *And the dreams that you dare to dream,*
> *Really do come true. . ."*

The unexpected, magnificent phenomenon of a rainbow also brings to mind the words of Victor Hugo, who wrote,

> *". . . Neither can a hand grasp a rainbow,*
> *But that doesn't diminish its power*
> *To nurture the hope of a meaningful life. . ."*

# Chapter Fifty-Two

# Acts of Kindness

There are altruistic and righteous personalities who perform heroic deeds and dedicate their lives to alleviating hardships endured by innocent human beings. It is fitting that one should remember such people. They have become my role models.

Fortunately, I have met many such individuals. The crucible of my life—from an early age—was influenced by well-meaning people who gave me the impetus to follow in their footsteps, setting examples for me in all my future endeavors. Throughout my life the law of Karma, an ethical principle of the Hindu religion, has impressed me; namely, that the previous acts of merit we perform will come back to us in our lifetime. This concept is also expressed in the universal Biblical adage, "As you sow, so shall you reap."

Even though the horror of Nazi persecution left me stateless, homeless, and penniless, I have been the grateful recipient of kindnesses bestowed on me by many good people. Because they extended a helping hand to me, I never felt hopeless or worthless. I have been poor but never had to sleep in the street. I have been hungry but never starved.

Through the years I have been frugal but never stingy, have slept in many beds, worn hand-me-down clothes, have eaten at different tables, and prayed in various synagogues around the world. In times of utter despair, countless human beings exhibited compassion and kindness, sharing their last crust of bread—even amid the trials and deprivations that befell the victims of Nazi oppression.

In Shanghai, after my mother died I felt like an orphan because I seldom saw my father, who worked long hours as a watchman at the other end of town. I appreciated the thoughtful people who sometimes invited my father and me for Shabbat or special occasions like a seder. In my travels as a young man in Sydney, I rarely needed to stay in hotels and from time to time enjoyed being a dinner guest of the hospitable Chief Rabbi.

Once in Los Angeles as a stranger, I entered an Orthodox synagogue only to say Kaddish on the anniversary of my father's death. I was invited to dinner after congregants learned I was a traveler.

I have tried to emulate those who helped me. After Eva and I arrived in California from South Bend, we were fortunate to stay with wonderful friends.

"If we ever own a home some day," I told Eva, "it must have a guest room so we can accommodate wayfarers and share with them our food, no matter how simple."

As a cantor, I have invited members of my temple and also out-of-town people to my home to continue the Jewish tradition modeled by Abraham's hospitality to strangers. Even when our home was very modest, we opened it to guests, many of whom graced our dinner table and stayed with us overnight. Today, owning a home in Palo Alto, I am thankfully able to continue extending such hospitality.

It didn't take me long to learn that the art of living is truly the art of giving. I'm sure we all can cite an event in our past when someone came to our aid in time of need. During many of my difficult days I was lucky to be showered with kindness and love from role models endowed with the spirit of giving. By encountering so many beautiful souls, my faith in humanity has been strengthened through belief in our fellow men.

The words of Eleanor Roosevelt ring in my ears:

*". . . Many people will walk in and out of your life. But only*
*True friends will leave footprints in your heart. . ."*

Doing things for others and being a caring friend has given me spiritual fulfillment. Through it, my reward has been finding real happiness.

*Chapter Fifty-Three*

# The Other Side of the Pulpit

In 1989 on the occasion of my twenty-fifth anniversary as cantor of Temple Beth Jacob, the congregation honored me at a tribute dinner. I was overwhelmed by the appreciation and congratulations extended to me. A special surprise, however, was the heartwarming appearance of Mrs. Hartwich, my beloved teacher in Germany and Shanghai. Already in her eighties, she spoke movingly about "the little boy from Berlin" who yearned to become a cantor.

Most Jewish people are probably not aware that the traditional name for a cantor (or hazzan) is "messenger of the congregation" or *Sheliach Tzibur* (a term denoted by the acronym *Shatz*). As a messenger of the congregation, the cantor is considered "a master of prayer with a trained voice" (a *Baal Tefilah*). This traditional name for a cantor explains the subtitle of my book, *Risen from the Ashes: Tales of a Musical Messenger.*

Many worshipers of our temple often have asked me, as a master of prayer, which are my favorites. I tell them the prayers I like best are all incorporated in a precious volume that has accompanied me throughout my life — the *Siddur*, the Jewish prayerbook. It contains hymns from the rabbis and poets along with prayers and supplications from the Torah and Talmud. I take the Siddur in my hand three times a day as I call on the Almighty to hear me. When I travel, my Siddur is the first item to be packed.

The words of the prayer book are set to music and chanted to a prescribed mode, reflecting the aspirations of the Jewish soul. Although these immortal words date back thousands of years, the Siddur has undergone many changes and updates including new additions, meditations on the Holocaust, and additional prayers for the establishment of the State of Israel.

Among my favorite prayers are the *Sh'ma* and *Veahavta*, which are recited twice a day. The *Veahavta* comes from the Book of Deuteronomy:

*". . . Love the Lord Your God with all your heart, with*
*all your soul, and with all your might. And these words*
*which I command you this day you shall take to heart.*
*You shall diligently teach them to your children. . .*
*recite them when you rise up in the morning and when*
*you lie down at night . . . and inscribe them upon the*
*doorposts of your houses and upon your gates. . ."*

Using the traditional Torah Trope (cantillation), the oldest form of Jewish music, I have taught the *Veahavta* chant to my congregation. Its words of undying faith have become my educational tool as we sing it in unison, proclaiming the duties incumbent on every Jew—to follow the Torah commandments and direct our hearts to God wherever we may be.

The *Veahavta* prayer is usually preceded by the *Sh'ma*, the watchword of Judaism which states, "Hear o Israel, the Lord our God, the Lord is One."

Another favorite that I have taught my students is a wonderful passage from the Talmud called *Elu Devarim* ("These are the duties . . ."). Still relevant today, it is a synopsis of the many commandments that the Torah declares can be performed without limit. This passage, found in the traditional prayerbook at the beginning of the morning service, is recited daily, and we sing it in the ancient *Gemara Nigun* (the traditional study mode).

*Elu Devarim*'s multiple duties (or commandments) include ". . . Honoring one's parents; doing deeds of loving kindness; attending the house of study punctually, morning and evening; providing hospitality; visiting the sick; helping the needy bride; probing the meaning of prayer; making peace between one person and another, and between man and wife. But the study of Torah is the most basic of them all. . ."

A beautiful evening prayer that goes back to Talmudic times is the *Hashkivenu*, which I love to chant with my temple choir. In translation it begins with "Cause us to lie down in peace" and asks for God's protection to keep us safe at night from all adversaries. *Hashkivenu* concludes with a metaphoric petition for peace from "the One who spreads out a tabernacle of peace over us, Israel and over Jerusalem."

Every Rosh Hashanah, the Jewish New Year, I am deeply moved when I render the *Hineni*, which means "Here I am." Known as the hazzan's prayer, *Hineni* is a poem of unknown authorship medieval in origin. It is deeply personal in nature and occurs at the beginning of the *Musaf* or additional service. This stirring recitative addressed to the Almighty proclaims that I, as messenger of the congregation, stand in awe as an emissary of His people.

*". . . I am a sinner, lacking good deeds, character and*
*piety and am asking for your mercy, to accept my*

*prayer as that of an elder with a pleasing countenance,*
*and the hope that my petition finds acceptance before*
*Your throne . . . Blessed are you who hearest prayer. . ."*

The High Holy Day congregation awaits the dramatic moment when, as is the traditional custom, I enter the sanctuary from the rear and begin chanting the *Hineni*.

"I really can't hear you when you're so far away from the microphone," complained a member who generally sits in the front row. "What's the reason for this custom?" he questioned.

I told him I don't have an answer, but I do know that the thousand worshipers sitting further back in the sanctuary enjoy my proximity when, as the *Sheliach Tzibur*, I pass close by them.

After researching the *Hineni* in the *Encyclopedia of Jewish Music* by Macy Nulman, however, I learned that in the 1800s a cantor named Joseph Altshul of Slonim in Eastern Europe apparently introduced that custom. As his choir stood waiting at the bimah, a singer would chant, "Where is the Cantor?"

"Here I am," he would respond from the rear of the synagogue.

"Why are you way back there at the doorway?" another singer would chant.

"Because I am poor in good deeds," was the cantor's humble reply as he made his way, chanting, down the aisle to his pulpit.

Today, the synagogue has been transformed into a community center where people come not only to pray, but to study, sing, and above all to meet each other. Synagogue duties have changed too. The rabbis in former days preached just twice a year, on the Sabbaths before Passover and Yom Kippur. In past times funerals were held only at the cemetery at the time of interment. Exceptions took place on rare occasions such as when renowned rabbis receive the privilege of a funeral service in the sanctuary prior to burial.

Weddings used to be held outdoors and Bar Mitzvahs were considered only added attractions to the regular Sabbath service. Nowadays, by contrast, the Temple is used for funerals, as a wedding chapel, and Bar and Bat Mitzvahs dominate the service with specially invited guests. Today Jews more often come to the synagogue rather than the cemetery to mourn loved ones who passed away. Submerged in memory and silent prayer, others come to celebrate and honor the holy Sabbath.

During my career another dimension of Jewish music has greatly influenced me, one that I attribute to my good friend of blessed memory Shlomo Carlebach. Known as the Singing Rabbi, he was born into a prominent rabbinical family in Berlin. A beloved composer of hundreds of Hassidic prayer melodies—real Jewish soul music—he told stories as he sang, accompanying himself on the guitar.

Shlomo joined me several times in concerts at Beth Jacob. I was deeply saddened when he passed away in 1994 at the young age of sixty-nine. His "Am Yisrael Hai," "Eyn Keloheynu," and "Eso Enai" are sung the world over and have become new classics. When I play my guitar and sing Shlomo's songs, the whole congregation joins in.

Synagogue life has been changed by the September 11 tragedy. No longer safe havens for meditation and prayer, synagogues have routine security and police protection while people are often nervous going into a house of worship. But we must not be deterred by anti-Semitism and terrorists who want to destroy us; we must continue to preserve the institution of the synagogue.

The prayers both in the Siddur and in the sacred Book of Ecclesiastes encompass all our human experiences, including both joy and fear. I cherish the inspiring words attributed to King Solomon:

> "... *For everything there is a season*
> *and a time for every purpose under the heaven.*
> *A time to be born and a time to die;*
> *A time to weep and a time to laugh;*
> *A time to mourn and a time to dance;*
> *A time to be silent and a time to speak. . ."*

When chanting I stand alone and exposed. With my God-given instrument, a human voice with the gift of melody, I attempt to satisfy all in attendance. But that is a service that inspires and also enhances the emotional appeal of the music.

I have been grappling for some time with introducing new music but I understand that by and large what people call "traditional" Jewish music is simply what is most familiar to them. By dividing the music into three categories, I try to strike some kind of balance between congregational participation, choir selections for spiritual listening, and my own solo presentations. In most cases I believe I succeed, but my responsibility is great and the time element is also important.

"Is the service too long?" I recently asked a temple member.

"Not really," was the answer, "it just seems long."

Once a congregant cornered me. "Cantor, I just love when you sing the closing hymn *Adon Olam.*"

I got the hint and answered politely, "I suppose you prefer more congregational singing?"

"Oh no," he replied jokingly, "It's just that when you sing *Adon Olam,* I know it's almost time for coffee and cookies in the social hall!"

## Chapter Fifty-Four

# On Retirement

It is with hesitation that I call this chapter "Retirement" because the term generally connotes a negative image. For me personally, the word suggests a state of being tired. Since I couldn't come up with a better word to describe my present point in life, I consulted a thesaurus for something more appropriate and found other terms—regression, recession, relinquishment, and resignation. Such alternatives do not at all describe my situation, which I perceive as a fine and fortunate state.

When I was younger, the thought of compulsory retirement at age sixty-five was abhorrent. I carried on indefatigably, barely noticing the fleeting years, so busy from morning till night that I was oblivious of time passing. Many of us fortunate enough to be healthy seem unaware that aging eventually takes its toll. And when it does, some people long for the proverbial Fountain of Youth, which reminds me of an anecdote about the young Picasso's famous portrait of Gertrude Stein. Ms. Stein, it is said, was dissatisfied, complaining that the painting made her look old.

"But you *will be old* eventually," Picasso replied nonchalantly.

Indeed, he was right, we will all be old sooner or later. In the course of time, my hair turned grayish, numerous wrinkles have invaded my face, my movements prefer a slower pace, and my short term-memory is not what it used to be. Often I misplace items I just had in my hand and then retrace my steps to find them again. Lately, I've resorted to writing things down when planning my agenda for the day, but in spite of everything I still feel young at heart and am inspired by studying the lives of individuals who—in spite of old age—achieved heights of creativity.

When Verdi was eighty he wrote the opera *Falstaff*. Goethe completed his masterpiece *Faust* also at eighty. Arthur Rubinstein was almost ninety when he gave his final concert in London. Pablo Casals, the world's greatest cellist, played a concert at the White House when he was eighty-six, and in his nineties he practiced five hours a day.

Grandma Moses began painting at the age of seventy-eight after her fingers became stiff from embroidering. She lived to be 101 years old. Jack Lalanne, the well known fitness guru, is eighty-nine and still pumps iron every day. At ninety-six George Bernard Shaw supposedly was pruning a tree, fell out, and fractured his leg. Compared to such paragons I am just an ordinary person, but they have become my role models and I try to emulate them.

In 1995 at the age of sixty-nine, I resigned from my congregation as cantor, not in order to disappear, but rather to simply slow down and enjoy my happy life with Eva by traveling, singing the songs I like, and doing some lecturing and tutoring. But my bout with throat cancer and Eva's tragic death of lung cancer changed all that. My cancer surgery left me with a speech impediment that makes it difficult to deliver presentations; however, I still am able to sing and lead services.

Although I'm fortunate to have survived a life-threatening illness, Eva's death left me with an indelible scar that demanded a big adjustment. As a result, I had to reinvent myself to find new meaning in life.

I began reading all the self-help books I could get my hands on, becoming interested in alternative medicine and other body-mind theories as factors that contribute to good health. Basically, all these approaches agree that when it comes to aging, the primary principle is to enhance the quality of one's life, which I do by keeping busy.

Music and writing have furthered my own healing, and prayer has deepened my spirituality. Meditation is part of my daily diet along with good nutrition. To avoid stress I practice Yoga and go regularly to the YMCA for stretching and exercise. I try to relax with a good book or listen to classical music. Laughter is good therapy and a sense of humor helps me maintain a cheerful attitude.

I still welcome a good joke and put the best ones on file. I don't jog anymore, but I still enjoy riding my bicycle. Three times a year I travel as chaplain on Princess Line cruises to conduct Jewish services, see the world, and meet interesting people. My faithful companion Nina now joins me. Above all, though, I study the Bible regularly. The teachings of the prophet Isaiah inspire me:

> ". . . But they that wait for the Lord shall renew their strength;
> They shall mount up with wings as eagles;
> They shall run, and not be weary;
> They shall walk and not faint. . ."

Although I know and accept my limitations, ever since I retired I've been busier than ever. It sounds like a cliché, but it's true. Far from slowing down or withdrawing from creativity, I now have the freedom to choose how to spend the sunset of my life. During nearly fifty years of conducting services in the synagogue, I vividly recall the times I stood before the open ark on Yom Kippur and recited *Shema Kolenu* (Hear Our Prayer), which marks a solemn plea for mercy. Based on Psalm 71, the prayer includes a verse referring to old age, which I have only recently begun to comprehend:

> *". . . Do not cast us away from your presence;*
> *Do not remove your holy spirit.*
> *Do not dismiss us when we are old;*
> *As our strength diminishes, do not abandon us. . ."*

Victor Frankl, the psychiatrist, endured Nazi atrocities but survived the Auschwitz concentration camp. After immigrating to the United States, he became a professor and author, remaining active into his nineties. His famous book *Search for Meaning* has been translated into fourteen languages. An analyst of human behavior, Frankl recommends that people spend their free time in purposeful activity. I agree. As a volunteer in my congregation, my greatest mitzvah is to visit the sick in the hospital. When I look around, I always discover someone who is much worse off than I am.

An article on "Healing through Writing" in the *Coping with Cancer* magazine prompted me to take a creative writing class, which gave me the impetus to tell my story. I began to write this book in the hope of being remembered by my children, grandchildren, and the many friends who have urged me to share my experiences. Friendship is very meaningful to me, and I cherish the few good, real friends who want to hear my stories.

*Chapter Fifty-Five*

# Shanghai Revisited

In 2002 after a span of sixty-two years, I returned for the first time to the Far East. I was engaged to conduct Passover services on a *Regal Princess* cruise, so Nina and I flew to China and spent four days in Beijing, where the cruise originated.

After stops in Sydney, South Korea, Pusan, and Nagasaki the ship on March 31 returned to China and sailed into Shanghai, where we planned a five-day visit. At the prospect of seeing Shanghai again, I was filled with nervous anticipation and spent a sleepless night. As the ship pulled into the harbor at 6 A.M., I stood on the deck, remembering that the main purpose of my trip was not only returning to the city of my youth but also finding my mother's tombstone.

After so many years, my first glimpse of Shanghai was a city enveloped in a hazy, smoggy gray sky. Somewhat teary-eyed and filled with emotion, I again saw the Bund, the elegant waterfront boulevard that is still Shanghai's most famous landmark. In the distance, skyscrapers painted a scenic panorama resembling New York City. Just as Nina and I prepared to go ashore, the ship's purser surprised us.

"You can't get off the ship until you get a new visa," he warned. "China is a Communist country and you may not be able to obtain another one on short notice."

Obtain another visa? But we already had one. In fact, I had paid fifty dollars for it. Nevertheless, the purser informed us that our visa had expired the same day we left Beijing. We had no warning that after visiting Japan we would need another one in order to return to China. How incongruous, I thought. In 1939 I entered Shanghai without any papers, but in 2002, under the Communist government, I needed a visa to get past Immigration.

After telling the official why I was returning to Shanghai, he promised to help, but said unconvincingly, "I'll see what I can do."

Meanwhile, from the deck of the *Regal Princess* I gazed at the Whangpoo (Yellow) River below, which was filled with cargo ships, sampans, houseboats and junks. It was reminiscent of the sights when I first came to Shanghai with my parents. But this time the water looked polluted. Across the river was Pudong, a giant development that today is Shanghai's Silicon Valley. It mushroomed in the last twenty years and seems to have sprung up from out of nowhere. It was just an empty, grassy marsh area when I left. Nearby Pudong was a breathtaking sight—a giant television tower, nicknamed "The Needle" with a rotating restaurant pointed heavenward.

After waiting for an hour, I returned to the Immigration counter to inquire about our visa situation. Several officers slowly arrived. Unperturbed, one by one they seated themselves at a table and began going over the visas, the passports, and the list of people waiting to enter Shanghai. Each officer lit up a cigarette although smoking was against the ship's rules. My blood pressure began an ascent when I discovered that my name was on the bottom of their list, which I saw was poorly organized and not arranged alphabetically.

After I paid a second fifty dollars for a new document, a smiling officer approached. He and the other officials began announcing the names of everyone whose visa was completed, but in between names, they drank coffee, talked, and continued smoking. Finally they called my name.

"You're cleared," the purser said. "Enjoy yourself ashore."

With a sigh of relief, my blood pressure returned to normal.

At the port we were greeted by a guide, Chamutal Ben Bassat, whom I had arranged for previously in the States. A van with driver waited for us and we were joined by three other passengers on a sightseeing tour.

Our first stop was Hongkew (now called Hongkou), the area formerly designated for stateless refugees. As in previous days, Hongkou is still a poor district. The old familiar Eastern Theater, the movie house I so often frequented, was still there but somewhat dilapidated. I recalled that when the Jewish community rented the theater for High Holy Day services, the Eastern was converted into a temporary synagogue. On weekends, the top of the theater, the Mascot Roof Garden, was used as a coffee house with entertainment and dancing to a fine orchestra.

Walking along Changyang Lu (formerly called Wayside Road) and observing some of the old houses, I saw that little had changed except for store facelifts. Traffic was still horrendous. Pedal-pushing rickshaws, bicycles, motor scooters, taxis and honking buses mingled with pedestrians, who appeared oblivious to traffic signals. A number of people wore white surgical masks to protect against Shanghai's severe air pollution.

Chamutal took us to Dalian Road (formerly called Chusan Road), where I once worked as a cook at Sida's restaurant. One can still see the old decrepit buildings, newly refurbished only at the entrance, and decorated with laundered sheets and underwear hanging like banners from the windows. One woman was washing clothes in front of her house. Another, seated on the sidewalk, was offering some medication for sale. Dressed like a nurse in a white gown, she set out a little table covered in front with paraphernalia for taking a customer's blood pressure.

We walked to the Ohel Moshe Synagogue at 62 Chang Yang Road (formerly called Ward Road). The building appeared unchanged and in fairly good condition, but it is now a museum under the control of the People's Republic of China. A plaque by the synagogue entrance states it was built in 1927 by Russian Jews who had arrived earlier, escaping the Bolshevik Revolution. At the doorway stands a sculpture of Moses, a gift from an American Hadassah chapter.

Entering the old synagogue, I was filled with memories, as I stood once more on the very spot where I became a Bar Mitzvah at the age of fourteen. In front of the now-empty ark of the Torahs, I again chanted from memory a few of the same *Haftorah* verses that I had sung in 1940.

A highlight of my visit to the synagogue was meeting Mr. Wang Fa Liang, eighty-one, the gentleman in charge of the museum. As a child, he too had lived in the Jewish ghetto. He welcomed me in fine English, his green eyes gleaming in delight and a happy smile on his wrinkled face.

"We had a good relationship with the Jewish people," he said, telling how everyone made friends and lived together in harmony. "They did their business and we did ours. We also suffered miserably under the Japanese occupation. Just like you."

Inviting us to meet his wife and family, Mr. Wang took us across the street to his extremely modest home. *Deja vu* struck me as we entered the apartment, which he shared with his children. His tiny bedroom, although spotless, contained only a large bed, night table, bookcase, and an old TV set. In the adjacent hallway his son was cooking a meal on a charcoal stove, the same kind I myself had once cooked on.

I was impressed later when our guide explained that part of the proceeds from our tour helped the Wang family financially especially since their apartment, built in prewar days, was soon to be torn down and replaced by a public housing development.

Coming to the center of town, we crossed over the Soochow Creek via the Garden Bridge, and it felt almost like coming from Hunter's Point to San Francisco. Hongkou was still rundown, but then suddenly an entirely different picture came into view—one with skyscrapers. As a teenager I used to ride my bicycle over the Garden Bridge while a Japanese soldier stood guard in the center. Since he was a symbol of the emperor, I had to get off, bow, walk past him and only then resume my ride. Failure to do so invited dire consequences.

Our van took us along the waterfront to the Bund and Freedom Park. Huge crowds were promenading, enjoying goodies sold by street vendors. A new underpass to avoid traffic crossed beneath the boulevard to Nanking Road, Shanghai's main street. The luxurious Peace Hotel (formerly Cathay) built by the tycoon David Sassoon, again welcomes international guests as in its former glory. Exquisitely dressed women do their shopping. Gone are the pigtails and bound feet as well as the subsequent drab Mao jackets. No shortages were evident, and the stores are filled with imported goods, the latest fashions and the finest confections.

Shanghai, a sleeping city in recent decades, is reinventing itself. The construction crane seems to be the city's national bird. The present population of sixteen million is constantly growing as thousands of newcomers, dreaming of a brighter future, arrive daily from the interior to seek work.

An especially memorable tour was our visit to Houshan Park (formerly Wayside Park). There stood the only monument in all of China that commemorates the existence of the Jewish ghetto. Bearing witness to our past was the memorial erected by the city in 1993 and dedicated when Yitzhak Rabin, then Prime Minister of Israel, visited Shanghai. Written in three languages—Chinese, English, and Hebrew—it is a tribute to all who lived there, and it recounts the lives of the stateless refugees who fled Nazi persecution and came to Shanghai from 1937 to 1941.

While reading the inscription, I was suddenly surrounded by a number of curious, elderly Chinese. A crowd gathered and listened in amazement when I began speaking in broken Chinese. With the help of some translators, I told about my sojourn in Shanghai as a youngster and how thankful I was to have found a haven to survive the Hitler era.

Retracing my earlier footsteps in Shanghai, I recalled again the day my mother died of amoebic dysentery, and I still remembered the spot where she was buried. I had fervently hoped to find her old tombstone, which weathered so many storms since it was salvaged out of the Hongkew rubble. But my endeavor was impossible. After China took over the whole city, the four Jewish cemeteries were removed so none exist today. My mother's remains, I'm sure, were among the eliminated graves. Although I was told that a few cemetery relics could still be found in the outskirts of Shanghai, the day of her death has gone into oblivion and her burial place has vanished. I can, however, still recite the Memorial Prayer, and that has to be sufficient because the memory of my mother is permanently enshrined in my heart and will always be with me. Even though I didn't find her tombstone, the monument in the park put up by the city government was a fitting testimony to the twenty thousand Jews who lived in the Shanghai Ghetto.

In 2004 an article appeared in the *New York Times* featuring Christopher Choa, a New York architect who moved to Shanghai. He became fascinated with the story of the Jewish ghetto during World War II. After learning about the planned redevelopment of this rundown area by the city government, he became concerned about the potential loss to posterity. He felt "The history of the Jews in Shanghai is so compelling that it is worth preserving."

A company was formed by two Canadian Jews and Mr. Choa to raise $400 million dollars for restoring and preserving some of the historical buildings. Architects, developers, and the Chinese government are discussing the future of the old Shanghai Ghetto, an area presently called the North Bund. Perhaps the Ohel Moshe Synagogue, the Eastern Theater, and other buildings will remain as reminders to residents and tourists of the important history of this area.

One plan even includes bringing in gravestones of Jewish residents from former cemeteries. In that way not only the Ghetto but also the life of my mother and those of other Ghetto Jews will always be remembered.

The Hongkou Ghetto, once an asylum to save twenty thousand stateless refugees is just a memory. After five decades, a rebirth of Jewish life is taking place, although Judaism is not officially recognized by the Chinese Communist government. Our guide told us that for the first time High Holiday services were permitted to take place in the newly restored Ohel Rachel Synagogue. There are presently 250 Jews in Shanghai. Shalom Greenberg, of the Hassidic tradition is the full time rabbi. Shabbat services are usually held in hotel rooms or private homes.

I leave Shanghai and memories of bygone days echo in my heart. I came here as a boy, stateless, to remain in a waiting room of exile. My parents are long gone. With gratitude I return to the Regal Princess, anchored on the Whangpoo River, proudly, with an American passport in my hand, to continue my journey to Hong Kong.

I proceed to the ship's computer to send an e-mail to my children describing my visit. Words from the Bible come to my mind:

> *"One generation goes and another comes,*
> *But the earth endures forever."*

# Chapter Fifty-Six

# Reflections on Identity

Now at seventy-nine years of age, I look back on my life, reflecting who I am and who I have been.

It seems that between years of living on the edge and sailing the oceans over four continents, I have had many different identities. In Germany, I was a citizen of Berlin. In Shanghai I was a stateless refugee and a penniless, motherless boy. I was also a cook, a Bar Mitzvah, a talented singer, and a stowaway. In Melbourne and Sydney I was an illegal alien, a fugitive, a chef, and an imposter. After coming to Los Angeles in 1947, I attained even more identities—legal immigrant, leader of Jewish services, soldier. And later—husband, citizen, father, restaurant owner, student, singing waiter, graduate, cantor, educator.

In repeated attempts to make a place for myself while residing in Germany, China, Australia, America, and for brief periods in Israel, I have vivid memories—both happy and unhappy. Since the end of World War II, I have traversed the whole world, toured every continent, met and interacted with countless people, learned many languages, and studied the musical history of each country I visited.

When Eva and I brought Jewish Stanford students to Germany, I conducted a memorial service at Bergen Belsen, the former concentration camp and also in Berlin, the city of my birth. German non-Jewish friends took me to the section where I lived with my parents at *Babelsbergerstrasse* 47. I didn't recognize the rebuilt house and the tree-lined street. In front, a lilac bush in full bloom gave forth a nostalgic fragrance. Well-dressed women pushed baby carriages, and children played hopscotch on the sidewalk.

The sound of the German language reverberated in my ears. My friends expected me to be emotional, reliving my childhood, but I stood in silence, stone-faced, taking it all in but feeling unmoved by the encounter. The following day, on Sabbath morning, something did happen when I attended services at the Pestalozzistrasse synagogue.

Before the Torah reading, I beheld the cantor standing in front of the open ark, clutching the Torah in his arms, singing the *Sh'ma Yisroel* (Hear, O Israel!). When he chanted in the same traditional melody I grew up with, suddenly tears filled my eyes and only then did I begin to reminisce. The Jewish music, the German language, my mother tongue with its beautiful poetry and literature was reawakened in me.

Then I said to myself, this is my home. But something was missing. I don't really belong here.

After our German visit, Eva and I spent the following summer in Israel. Although I had visited many times, I never grew tired of coming again. Jerusalem, my favorite city, attracted me. I wasn't born in Israel, nor did I have family to warrant my remaining there, but during the past thirty-five years I spent three Sabbaticals in this little country. It was there that I perfected my Hebrew, teaching it to students in the United States. Israel is the cradle of my religion with its holidays, the music of my people, the country of my ancestors, and the land of the Bible.

I said to myself, this is my home. Yet again there was something missing.

More than half a century ago I entered America, arriving in San Francisco at the age of twenty-one with eighty dollars in my pocket. The land of democracy and freedom opened her doors to me but my European background and culture was and is still a strong influence. I must admit that I've never been to a baseball or football game. I'm embarrassed that I don't even know the rules of the games, having been a soccer player as a child. I'm happy to experience a touchdown only when flying by air and landing safely at my destination. I wasn't raised on turkey and cranberry sauce, apple or pumpkin pie. Halloween and Thanksgiving are still a bit foreign to me. Hot dogs leave me cold. For dinner I'd prefer a Wiener Schnitzel and for dessert a Napoleon slice.

I feel blessed and thankful to America. I never finished high school yet was able to obtain a higher education, a bachelor's degree, cantorial ordination, a master's degree in education from Stanford, and an honorary doctorate in music from Hebrew Union College. I was fortunate to serve my congregation, Temple Beth Jacob, with distinction for thirty-five years.

For me the American Dream has become a reality. As a proud American citizen I vote, I worship as I please, I'm fully integrated, I'm comfortable, and I own a beautiful home in Palo Alto, California. I've acquired many friends and have fine neighbors. I greet each new day thankful to be alive, to have survived unscathed, and to have risen from the ashes. My Jewish religion has given me faith, love and courage to share my blessings with others. My destiny has brought me to these shores, and I know I am not going anywhere else. Yet, I say to myself, am I really at home? Even here I feel there is still something missing.

The words of Plato have been my guiding light.

> *". . . Life is a search for wisdom,*
> *A search for beauty and*
> *A search for truth. . ."*

After many vicissitudes and wanderings, I still ponder how to define *identity*. Is it a sense of belonging? To this day, my question is still—*where do I really belong?*

My answer would have to agree with Marcus Aurelius, the Second Century Roman emperor and philosopher who said,

> *"I am a citizen of the world."*

## Chapter Fifty-Seven

# Epilogue

Much credit for my writing this book goes to my children, who motivated me, and to my six grandchildren, who were fascinated hearing stories about my past nomadic life. For them I endeavored to awaken both the many happy and unhappy adventures I experienced. By recalling events from my early childhood to the present day, I realized that every person has enough life experiences to tell a story, not only the rich and famous.

Reviewing all I have experienced in recent years, the worst thing was having throat cancer. It was life threatening, but I didn't lose my life; I just lost part of my tongue. Cancer taught me to use my spiritual resources and face affliction with hope, courage, and faith in God. As for my eating problem, I adopted the philosophy of the French playwright Moliere who said, "We eat to live and not live to eat." Life is a heavenly gift that requires constant adjustment—and I have adjusted to accepting things as they are, making the best of it all, and finding a purpose to go on.

Not long after my illness, another shocking event occurred. When I lost Eva to lung cancer, a part of me died along with her. As my children tried to ease my pain, I grew even closer to them, and in my solitude after Eva's death, I found that taking up the pen lifted my spirits. But I was lonely. We read in Genesis:

> *". . . It is not good that man should be alone;*
> *I will make a companion to suit him. . ."*

The stress of being alone, especially at night, gnawed at my heart, causing depression. Then I met my companion—Nina Baller Lobban. A piano teacher, Nina is the daughter of Adolph Baller, whom I knew from my Stanford days. Besides being a piano professor, he was the accompanist for

Yehudi Menuhin. A superb musician, with his wife who also escaped from Nazis in 1939, Adolph Baller coached me at one time in Schumann's song cycle "Dichterliebe," set to the poems by Heinrich Heine. Nina and I have much in common. She also speaks a fluent German, loves chamber music, and has generously provided piano accompaniment for some of my songs. Her warmth and caring personality has eased my loneliness and brightened my spirits.

In my lifetime I have witnessed many historic events and changes. Now especially since I am retired, I often find myself reflecting on some contemporary problems.

As a teacher and educator, I'm concerned about the calamitous effects of the financial problems confronting our schools. Arts and music are being cut while surely it is song and dance that can play a role to help create harmony and unite us globally. Physical education is drastically curtailed at the very time when too many young people are becoming obese and need to be involved in sports programs. I can't stress enough how important it is for students to learn foreign languages, yet language arts are being slashed. In my travels I have been able, because I know several languages, to communicate with and meet interesting new people.

All the technological progress in the last decades, unfortunately, has advanced neither our moral behavior nor our consciousness that as God's children, each of us is a unique human creation. By teaching only facts and information, we neglect spiritual aspects like love and self-worth. Scripture tells us "there is nothing new under the sun," a statement that helps explain the renewed interest in spirituality and the research supporting the powerful mind-body relationship. These ideas can be traced to ancient concepts that have always existed in Judaism, including Kabalah and Jewish mysticism. Such teachings have exhilarated me.

I am deeply disturbed that resurgent anti-Semitism is once again causing fear among Jews and insecurity among Israelis. Synagogues and cemeteries are still desecrated throughout the world. An Israeli athlete boycotted by Iranians in the 2004 Olympics is today's variation of the same racial hatred exhibited in the 1936 Olympics, which I witnessed, and the 1972 Olympics in which Israeli athletes were slaughtered.

In the Arab world, intense hatred of Israel and Jews is typified by Iran's response to its recent earthquake, declaring that it's preferable for their citizens to die in the wreckage rather than accept rescue assistance from Israel. Anti-Semitism has become so "politically correct" that the French ambassador to England, in diplomatic circles, can get away with describing Israel, the only democracy in the Middle East, as "nothing but a shitty little country."

I am dismayed by the amount of violence worldwide as well as local. Here in the San Francisco Bay Area alone, there are hate crimes and killings every day. I don't want or need a gun, though others, including some Jewish families, feel they must possess weapons. I was brought up to despise violence although I grew up during the most vicious period of the twentieth century.

My father had a pistol from his service in the German army, but he always kept it locked up. When Hitler came to power, my mother feared Nazi searches because it was dangerous for Jews to possess weapons. One night she concealed in her purse my father's gun and threw it into the Spree River. I share my mother's aversion to guns, but when I was in the U.S. Army I learned to shoot and kill—if necessary.

I survived one Holocaust and have wondered if another can occur again. Yes, it can. At the moment it is occurring in the Sudan. The United Nations does so little to protest. I am thinking of Pastor Martin Niemoller, a Protestant clergyman in Germany who died in 1984. He was arrested in Berlin in 1937 for opposing anti-Semitism and spent the rest of the war in a concentration camp. He wrote,

*". . . First the Nazis came for the communists and I didn't speak up because I was not a communist. Then they came for the Jews, and I didn't speak up because I was not a Jew. Then they came for the Trade Unionists and I didn't speak up because I was not a Trade Unionist. Then they came for the Catholics, and I was a Protestant so I didn't speak up. Then they came for me – and there was no one left to speak up for me."*

Niemoller's words are a reminder that we cannot sit idly by. Our turbulent world is filled with injustice, terror, hatred, and strife, yet we must not lose hope; we must learn to work together. I believe there are no limitations on what we as individuals can do to meet the many challenges of our ailing universe. However, I don't agree with the prophets of doom who claim that the world is going to self-destruct. I choose to be optimistic. My roller coaster existence never caused me to lose hope in providence of better days.

In recent years I have deepened my commitment to bringing happiness to others by extending help and hope to those less fortunate. My aim is to return a measure of the empathy and kindness that others have extended to me over the years. I'm not resting on my laurels, but trying in my own little way to continue to have faith in both God and humanity. I believe that each one of us needs to be involved in our community in some small way by, for example, helping others, electing good leaders, and doing whatever we can to leave the world a better place than we found it. In the community I speak at schools about racism and the Holocaust; at my synagogue I volunteer to conduct Bar and Bat Mitzvahs, serve as cantor, and read Torah.

I am grateful that my career has provided me the opportunity to make a difference in the world. I have been privileged to train a thousand Bar and Bat Mitzvah students, many of whom have become prominent, productive people, including fourw rabbis and many physicians. As a teacher of Judaism I have tried to reach out and use my musical gift to bring joy and healing. I have been invited to share both sad and joyous occasions of my students, who still keep in touch with me through pictures and letters.

In spite of my age and physical shortcomings, I have not allowed cancer to rob me of a future. I enjoy life and look forward to many new milestones ahead. Continuing to conduct religious services as chaplain on cruise ships still gives me great pleasure and now Nina accompanies me. On formal nights during a cruise, when we're seated at the ship's dining table, I wear my faithful tuxedo—the one I purchased long ago as a student in New York. It still fits me, it's well preserved and aside from cruises, it hangs patiently in my closet, awaiting the next auspicious occasion. Sometimes when an invitation arrives for a black tie optional wedding or Bar Mitzvah, I wonder what to wear but then I usually choose my tuxedo.

After my cancer surgery I felt trepidation, especially about speaking to cruise passengers, so I used to preface my remarks by explaining that although my speech isn't what it once was, I hope they will understand me. And they do. In fact, after every trip I get fan mail from passengers saying they enjoy and are inspired by my music, the Shabbat services, and the stories I tell about my life, especially my early years.

As a child, when I was kicked out of Germany, I carried one suitcase and at the Italian border was strip-searched by Nazis, who hated both democracy and Jews. I had no hidden valuables for them to steal and my God-given talent of a beautiful voice was something they couldn't take away from me.

On a recent return trip from a cruise in Italy, I again carried one suitcase. Before getting on the plane I was strip-searched, a protection against terrorism and other people today who also hate both democracy and Jews. This time, though, I wasn't being kicked out. I was carrying a U.S. passport and coming home as an American with a melody in my heart.

> "... America, America
> God shed his grace on thee
> And crown thy good with brotherhood
> From sea to shining sea. . ."

I am thankful to live in this beautiful country. I have truly found the American dream. Today I can sit and meditate in my garden and decorate my house with the flowers I grow. I'm retired but I'm not disappearing. I close with the words of an anonymous poet:

> *". . . I looked for my god, but my God I could not see.*
> *I looked for my soul, but it eluded me.*
> *I looked for my brother and sister, then I found all three. . ."*